French Phrase Book

French translation by
Andrée Chamings

French Phrase Book

Edmund Swinglehurst

NEWNES·BOOKS

NEWNES·BOOKS

First published in 1979 by
The Hamlyn Publishing Group Limited
Published in 1983 by Newnes Books,
an imprint of The Hamlyn Publishing Group Limited,
Bridge House, 69 London Road, Twickenham,
Middlesex TW1 3SB, England

© Copyright The Hamlyn Publishing Group Limited 1979
and Newnes Books 1983

Ninth Impression 1986

ISBN 0 600 33608 5

Printed in Great Britain by
Hazell Watson & Viney Limited,
Member of the BPCC Group,
Aylesbury, Bucks

Distributed in the U.S. by
Larousse & Co. Inc., 572 Fifth Avenue, New York,
New York 10036.

Contents

Introduction

The Newnes French Phrase Book is designed to help the
reader who has no previous knowledge of the language. With
its aid he should be able to make himself readily understood
on all occasions and to cope with the host of minor problems –
and some major ones – that can arise when on holiday or
travelling in France.

The key to successful speech in a foreign language is
pronunciation, and an outline of the principles of vowel and
consonant sounds and their usage in French is to be found at
the beginning of this book. This is followed by a section
dealing with the essential elements of French grammar. A
close study of these two sections and constant reference to
them will be of the utmost value: with the pattern of sentence
construction in mind and a feeling for the sound of the
language, the reader will be well equipped to use the phrases
in this book.

These are set out in logical order, beginning with the various
means of travel and entry to the country. The section on
accommodation covers the whole range from hotels and
private houses and villas to youth hostels and camping sites.
Particular attention is paid in the chapter on eating and
drinking to the speciality dishes and wines from the different
regions which have made French cuisine famous throughout
the world. Shopping, too, is covered in detail; whether the
reader wishes to indulge in a shopping spree of chic French
fashions or equip his self-catering apartment with a week's
supply of groceries, he will find a selection of appropriate
phrases easy to refer to and simple to use.

Entertainment, sightseeing, public services, and general
conversations in the hotel bar are all covered, and there is an

important section of commercial and banking phrases of particular value to the businessman. In addition to carefully chosen phrases, each section includes an appropriate vocabulary which is as comprehensive as possible, and at the end of the book there are quick-reference metric conversion tables for the more important temperatures, weights and measures.

The Newnes French Phrase Book will not only enable the traveller to handle any situation with confidence but will help to make his stay in France a more enjoyable one.

Guide to French Pronunciation

This is intended for people with no previous knowledge of French and is based on English pronunciation. This means that it is not entirely accurate but the reader who pays careful attention to this section should, with practice, be able to make himself understood reasonably well in French.

The Vowels

Letter	Approximate Pronunciation	Example
a	between the *a* in bat and the *a* in rather	**ami, marcher**
é, er, ez	like the *a* in mate	**donné, étrange, porter, cherchez**
è, ê, e	like the *e* in set	**mère, être, avec**
e	like the *er* in father	**le, se, demander**
i	like *ee* in feet	**libre**
o	like *o* in pot	**mode, poste**
u	no exact English equivalent; round the lips to say '*oo*' and try to say '*ee*'. Close to sound of *ew* in few.	**rue, tuer, nu, vue**

Pronunciation

Vowel Sounds Written as Two or more Letters

ai, ay	like the *a* in mate	**j'ai, gai, pays**
aî, aient, ais, ait	like the *e* in set	**faîte, donnaient, marchais, voulait**
au, eau	like the *o* in dope	**chaud, beau**
ei	like the *e* in set	**veine**
eu	like the *e* in her	**veut, heure, seul**
oi	like *w* followed by the *a* in rather	**soi, doit**
ou	like *oo* in soon	**tout, roue**
ui	like the word *we*	**cuire, suit**

Nasal Vowels

These are vowels followed by *n* and occasionally by *m*. They are uttered through the nose and mouth at the same time and occur as single vowels or combinations of vowels as follows:

ain, ein, ien, in	like *ang* in sang without pronouncing the *g*	**bain, main, peint, rein, vient, bien, vin, linge**
an, en	like *alm* in calm	**banc, santé, entrer, vent**
on	like *ong* in song without pronouncing the *g*	**bon, ton, maison**
un	like *ung* in sung	**un, lundi, parfum**

The Consonants

LETTER	APPROXIMATE PRONUNCIATION	EXAMPLE
b, c, d, f, k, m, n, p, t, v, x, z	pronounced as in English	
ch	like *sh* in shop	**chaud**
ç	like *s* in sit	**garçon**
g	1 before *e* or *i* like *s* in leisure	**geste, gilet**
	2 elsewhere like *g* in go	**garçon, goût**
gn	like *ni* in onion	**peigne, vigne**
h	always silent in French	**heure, hôtel**
j	like *s* in leisure	**je, jour**
l	1 like *l* in late	**la, long**
ail(le), eil(le), euil(le), oeil, ueil(le)	2 like *y* in yet	**travail, soleil, feuille, fille**
qu	like *c* in cat	**qui, que**
r	1 trilled more than in English	**route, raison**
	2 silent in infinitives ending in *er*	**donner, manger**
s	1 usually like *s* in sit	**sage**
	2 between two vowels like *z* in size	**raison, visage**

3

Pronunciation

Liaison and Stress

The final consonants of French words are not usually
pronounced. However, if a word ending in a consonant is
followed by one beginning with a vowel, the consonant is
pronounced as though it were the first letter of the following
word. For example, in **les enfants sont arrivés** both the
s of **les** and the *t* of **sont** are pronounced.

French does not stress individual syllables of a word as
heavily as English does. Each syllable is stressed equally, with
just a slight emphasis on the last one.

A Little Grammar in Action

Nouns

All nouns in French are either masculine or feminine whether they refer to living beings or inanimate objects. The word for 'the' (or definite article) is **le** before a masculine noun and **la** before a feminine noun:

le lit the bed
le père the father
le garçon the boy

la maison the house
la femme the woman
la voiture the car

Although there are rules for knowing which nouns are masculine and which are feminine, the only way to be sure is to learn each noun with its definite article.

Before nouns beginning with a vowel or an *h* both **le** and **la** are shortened to **l'**:

l'arbre the tree
l'horloge the clock

In the plural most French nouns add an *s* (except those ending in -*s*, -*x* or -*z* which do not change), and the word for 'the' is **les** before both masculine and feminine nouns:

les lits the beds
les pères the fathers
les arbres the trees

les maisons the houses
les femmes the women
les horloges the clocks

Nouns ending in *-eau*, *-eu* and *-ou* usually add an *-x* to form the plural. Those ending in *-al* generally change their endings to *-aux* in the plural.

The word for 'a' is **un** before a masculine noun and **une** before a feminine noun:

un lit a bed
un garçon a boy

une maison a house
une voiture a car

The word for 'some' or 'any' is **du** before a masculine noun and **de la** before a feminine noun:

J'ai du pain I have some bread
Avez-vous de la viande? Have you any meat?

Before a noun beginning with a vowel or an *h* both **du** and **de la** become **de l'**:

Avez-vous de l'argent? Have you any money?
Il a de l'encre He has some ink

Before plural nouns, both masculine and feminine, 'some' or 'any' are translated by **des**:

Nous avons des cigarettes We have some cigarettes
Avez-vous des enfants? Have you any children?

In negative sentences **de** alone (**d'** before a vowel or an *h*) is used instead of **du**, **de la**, **de l'** or **des**:

Je n'ai pas de cigarettes I haven't any cigarettes
Nous n'avons pas de pain We have no bread
Il n'a pas d'enfants He has no children

The word for 'of' is **de** followed by the appropriate definite article or combined with it as follows:

le livre du garçon the boy's book
le toit de la maison the roof of the house
le chapeau de l'enfant the child's hat
les roues des voitures the wheels of the cars

Adjectives

The endings of adjectives depend on whether the noun they accompany is masculine, feminine or plural. Usually they add an *e* to make the adjective feminine and an *s* to make it plural.

le petit garçon the little boy
la maison verte the green house

les petits garçons the little boys
les maisons vertes the green houses

Note: in French, adjectives generally follow their nouns, but a few, like **petit** above, precede them.

Demonstrative Adjectives

The words for 'this', 'that', 'these' and 'those' are as follows:

ce garçon this or that boy
ces garçons these or those boys
cette maison this or that house
ces maisons these or those houses
cet enfant this or that child
ces enfants these or those children

Possessive Adjectives

The words for 'my', 'your', 'his', etc. change their form according to whether the noun they refer to is masculine, feminine or plural.

	MASCULINE	FEMININE	PLURAL
my	mon	ma	mes
your	ton	ta	tes
his/her/its	son	sa	ses
our	notre	notre	nos
your	votre	votre	vos
their	leur	leur	leurs

Grammar

Note: ton, etc. is the familiar form of 'your'. If you don't know people very well use **votre,** etc.

mon lit my bed
mes enfants my children

ton père your father
tes parents your parents

sa valise his or her suitcase
ses mains his or her hands

son chien his or her dog
ses clés his or her keys

notre voiture our car
nos voitures our cars

votre livre your book
vos livres your books

leur maison their house
leurs maisons their houses

Personal Pronouns

The words for 'I', 'you', 'he', etc. are as follows:

1 When used as the subject of a verb:

je chante I sing
tu chantes you sing
il chante he sings
elle chante she sings
nous chantons we sing
vous chantez you sing
ils chantent they sing (masc.)
elles chantent they sing (fem.)

2 When used as the direct object of a verb:

Monsieur Dupont me connaît	Mr Dupont knows me
te	you
le	him
la	her
nous	us
vous	you
les	them

3 When used as the indirect object of a verb:

Monsieur Dupont me parle	Mr Dupont speaks to me
te	you
lui	him
lui	her
nous	us
vous	you
leur	them

These pronouns are always placed in front of the verb.

4 When used after a preposition:

Ces fleurs sont pour moi	These flowers are for me
toi	you
lui	him
elle	her
nous	us
vous	you
eux (masc.)	them
elles (fem.)	them

Remember that **tu** is the familar form of 'you'. **Vous** is the correct pronoun to use when talking to people you do not know very well.

Verbs

The whole subject of French verbs is too complicated for detailed discussion in a phrase book but for the traveller who wants a quick grasp of verbs with which he can communicate while travelling in French-speaking countries the following basic rules will be useful.

Regular Verbs

Most French verbs are regular in their formation and fall into one of three categories:

1 Verbs ending in *-er* in the infinitive

donner	to give
je donne	I give
tu donnes	you give
il donne	he gives
/elle	/she
nous donnons	we give
vous donnez	you give
ils donnent	they give
/elles	

2 Verbs ending in *-ir* in the infinitive

finir	to finish
je finis	I finish
tu finis	you finish
il finit	he finishes
/elle	/she
nous finissons	we finish
vous finissez	you finish
ils finissent	they finish
/elles	

3 Verbs ending in *-re* in the infinitive

vendre	to sell
je vends	I sell
tu vends	you sell
il vend	he sells
/elle	/she
nous vendons	we sell
vous vendez	you sell
ils vendent	they sell
/elles	

To form the negative of a verb **ne** is added before the verb and **pas** after it.

elle ne vend pas de fleurs she does not sell flowers

To ask a question, put the verb before the pronoun, use the phrase **est-ce que** or simply keep the normal order of words with a different intonation.

Voulez-vous mon livre?
Est-ce que vous voulez mon livre? } Do you want my book?
Vous voulez mon livre?

Irregular Verbs

The following are a few of the more useful common irregular verbs:

être	to be		**avoir**	to have
je suis	I am		**j'ai**	I have
tu es	you are		**tu as**	you have
il est	he is		**il a**	he has
/elle	/she		**/elle**	/she
nous sommes	we are		**nous avons**	we have
vous êtes	you are		**vous avez**	you have
ils sont	they are		**ils ont**	they have
/elles			**/elles**	

boire	to drink		**aller**	to go
je bois	I drink		**je vais**	I go
tu bois	you drink		**tu vas**	you go
il boit	he drinks		**il va**	he goes
/elle	/she		**/elle**	/she
nous buvons	we drink		**nous allons**	we go
vous buvez	you drink		**vous allez**	you go
ils boivent	they drink		**ils vont**	they go
/elles			**/elles**	

devoir	to have to		**dire**	to say
je dois	I must		**je dis**	I say
tu dois	you must		**tu dis**	you say
il doit	he must		**il dit**	he says
/elle	/she		/elle	/she
nous devons	we must		**nous disons**	we say
vous devez	you must		**vous dites**	you say
ils doivent	they must		**ils disent**	they say
/elles			/elles	

faire	to do, make		**mettre**	to put
je fais	I do		**je mets**	I put
tu fais	you do		**tu mets**	you put
il fait	he does		**il met**	he puts
/elle	/she		/elle	/she
nous faisons	we do		**nous mettons**	we put
vous faites	you do		**vous mettez**	you put
ils font	they do		**ils mettent**	they put
/elles			/elles	

partir	to leave		**pouvoir**	to be able
je pars	I leave		**je peux**	I can
tu pars	you leave		**tu peux**	you can
il part	he leaves		**il peut**	he can
/elle	/she		/elle	/she
nous partons	we leave		**nous pouvons**	we can
vous partez	you leave		**vous pouvez**	you can
ils partent	they leave		**ils peuvent**	they can
/elles			/elles	

prendre	to take		**savoir**	to know
je prends	I take		**je sais**	I know
tu prends	you take		**tu sais**	you know
il prend	he takes		**il sait**	he knows
/elle	/she		**/elle**	/she
nous prenons	we take		**nous savons**	you know
vous prenez	you take		**vous savez**	we know
ils prennent	they take		**ils savent**	they know
/elles			**/elles**	

venir	to come		**vouloir**	to want
je viens	I come		**je veux**	I want
tu viens	you come		**tu veux**	you want
il vient	he comes		**il veut**	he wants
/elle	/she		**/elle**	/she
nous venons	we come		**nous voulons**	we want
vous venez	you come		**vous voulez**	you want
ils viennent	they come		**ils veulent**	they want
/elles			**/elles**	

French Spoken

France, southern Belgium and western Switzerland form French-speaking Europe. Although each country speaks French with different accents, the phrases learnt from this book will be understood in all of them, as they will in the countries of the former French Empire.

France

The five most important towns of France epitomize the character of the region that surrounds them.

PARIS, although a cosmopolitan city, retains the princely character of the Ile de France – that rich agricultural basin through which the Seine flows and where royal courtiers once built their mansions.

LYONS on the Rhône sums up Burgundy, a land where cattle farms and vineyards produce the ingredients for the great restaurants of this region, and whose medieval churches and castles evoke the history of a once-independent kingdom.

BORDEAUX, the gastronomic rival of Burgundy, contains the great wine-producing châteaux, and the riches of the Atlantic coast, with its faint memories of ancient wars against the English. To the south lies the unspoilt region of the Dordogne, with its deep river gorges and remote villages.

NANTES to the north of Bordeaux is a gateway to Brittany, with its rugged coasts and mysterious woods, where the Arthurian legend still survives. This is the land of small fishing villages, delicious shellfish and **crêpes** – a Breton pancake.

MARSEILLES is in the south, which the French call the Midi.

This is the great sea port of the Mediterranean and the home of **bouillabaisse** – a dish of Mediterranean fish flavoured with the herbs that grow on the hills which tumble down to the sea. To the east lies the dazzling Côte d'Azur, with its elegant hotels, and to the west the fabulous Camargue.

Belgium

The French-speaking part of Belgium is in the south where the Walloon population live. To the north are the Flemish whose language is more akin to Dutch. A great trading nation since the Middle Ages, Belgium has many interesting towns, chief of which is the capital, Brussels.

Switzerland

Geneva and its lake are the centre of French-speaking Switzerland. This is a region of extensive vineyards and the mountainous valley of the upper Rhône. There are many famous resorts, including Lausanne and Montreux, along the lake, and the Castle of Chillon guards its eastern end.

Wherever you travel in these countries, you will find that a few words spoken in French will help to establish a friendly atmosphere.

Here to start with are some simple expressions of greeting and leave-taking:

Good morning.	**Bonjour.**
Good afternoon.	**Bonjour.**
Good evening.	**Bonsoir.**
Good night.	**Bonne nuit.**
How are you?	**Ça va?**
I'm very pleased to meet you.	**Enchanté.**

How do you do?	**Comment allez vous?**
Goodbye.	**Au revoir.**

Some words of courtesy:

Please.	**S'il vous plaît.**
Thank you.	**Merci.**
It's very kind of you.	**Vous êtes bien aimable.**
You are welcome.	**Je vous en prie.**
Not at all.	**De rien.**

And some questions:

Where is the hotel?	**Où est l'hôtel?**
What are you saying?	**Que dites-vous?**
When does the train leave?	**A quelle heure part le train?**
Who are you?	**Qui êtes vous?**
How much does it cost?	**C'est combien?**
Which is the road to . . . ?	**Quelle route faut-il-prendre pour . . . ?**
Why are we waiting?	**Pourquoi attendons-nous?**

Finally some useful common phrases:

Yes.	**Oui.**
No.	**Non.**
Why?	**Pourquoi?**
How?	**Comment?**
When?	**Quand?**
What?	**Comment?**
Where?	**Où?**

How much?	**Combien?**
How many?	**Combien?**
Please speak slowly.	**Parlez lentement s'il vous plaît.**
I do not understand French very well.	**Je ne comprends pas bien le français.**
Will you write it down, please?	**Pourriez-vous l'écrire s'il vous plaît?**
How do I say ...?	**Comment dit-on ...?**
What is the meaning of ...?	**Que veut dire ...?**
Please show me how this works.	**Pouvez-vous me faire voir comment cela fonctionne?**
How far is it to ...?	**A quelle distance se trouve ...?**
Where is the nearest ...?	**Où est le ... le plus proche?**
What time is it?	**Quelle heure est-il?**
Will you please help me?	**Pourriez-vous m'aider?**
Can you point to where we are on this map?	**Pouvez-vous m'indiquer sur la carte où nous nous trouvons?**
Which way do I go?	**Quelle direction faut-il prendre?**
Is there an official tourist office here?	**Y a-t-il un Syndicat d'Initiative ici?**
Where is the station/bus terminus/bus stop?	**Où est la gare/le terminus de l'autobus/l'arrêt de l'autobus?**
Where do I buy the tickets?	**Où achète-t-on les billets/les tickets?**

We have missed the train.	**Nous avons manqué le train.**
Do I turn right/left?	**Je tourne à droite/à gauche?**
Do I go straight ahead?	**Je vais tout droit?**
What is the name of this street?	**Comment s'appelle cette rue?**
How do I get to . . .?	**Pour aller à . . .?**
It is too expensive.	**C'est trop cher.**
Please give me the change.	**Donnez-moi la monnaie s'il vous plaît.**
I am tired.	**Je suis fatigué.**
I am hungry/thirsty.	**J'ai faim/soif.**
It is very hot/cold.	**Il fait très chaud/très froid.**
Please take me to my hotel.	**Pouvez-vous me conduire à l'hôtel?**
Is the service included?	**Le service est compris?**
Thank you very much.	**Merci beaucoup.**

And some idiomatic expressions:

Go away.	**Allez-vous en.**
Leave me alone.	**Laissez-moi tranquille.**
Shut up.	**Taisez-vous.**
How goes it?	**Ça marche?**
So so.	**Comme ci, comme ça.**
Don't move.	**Ne bougez pas.**
That's it.	**C'est ça.**
Carry on.	**Continuez.**

All Aboard

Journeys through French-speaking Europe are made easy by
the excellent means of communication and interesting
because of the centuries of history that have left their mark on
every town and village. Air travel is, of course, the quickest
way to get about and internal airlines provide an excellent
service, but journeys by train and coach or car are more
rewarding. Railways pass through beautiful scenery on some
routes such as the Paris–Brussels and Paris–Bordeaux, and
you can enjoy all the luxury of traditional train catering.

There are various kinds of train, classified according to speed
and the number of stops between termini. **T.E.E.** is the
Trans-Europe Express, a first-class, international train;
Rapide is an express; **Interville** is an inter-city train;
Express is a long-distance train; **Direct** a shorter-distance
stopping train. The **Omnibus** is the local train service,
sometimes provided by diesel autorails.

The roads are also well cared for and the autoroutes superb,
with good catering facilities as well as smooth road surfaces.
Service stations are plentiful and garages helpful. Best of all
are the little roads where travel is slow but every minute is a
joy if you are not in a hurry. This is where you reach the heart
of the country and where even a halting conversation can
create a warmth of communication.

Arrivals and Departures
Going through Passport Control and Customs

At most of the main gateway airports and ports there will be
someone with a smattering of English to help you, but you
cannot rely on this at all frontier posts. It is useful, therefore,
to know one or two basic phrases. Apart from making
communication easier, they help to establish a friendly

relationship with officials and often smooth the passage
through frontiers.

Good morning/afternoon/evening.	**Bonjour/bonjour/bonsoir.**
Here is my passport/visitor's card.	**Voilà mon passeport/ma carte d'identité.**
I am on holiday/on business.	**Je suis en vacances/en voyage d'affaires.**
I am visiting relatives/friends.	**Je vais voir des parents/des amis.**
The visa is on page …	**Le visa se trouve à la page …**
Here is my vaccination certificate.	**Voilà mon certificat de vaccination.**
They did not stamp my passport at the entry port.	**On ne m'a pas tamponné mon passeport au port d'arrivée.**
Will you please stamp my passport? It will be a souvenir of my holiday.	**Veuillez tamponner mon passeport. Ce sera un souvenir de vacances.**
I will be staying a few days/two weeks/a month.	**Je resterai quelques jours/deux semaines/un mois.**
I am just passing through.	**Je ne suis que de passage.**
My wife and I have a joint passport.	**Ma femme et moi avons un passeport commun.**
The children are on my wife's passport.	**Les enfants sont inscrits dans le passeport de ma femme.**
I didn't realize it had expired.	**Je ne m'étais pas rendu compte qu'il était périmé.**
Can I telephone the British Consulate?	**Je peux téléphoner au Consulat Britannique?**

I have nothing to declare.	Je n'ai rien à déclarer.
Do you want me to open my cases? Which one?	Voulez-vous que j'ouvre mes valises? Laquelle?
They are all personal belongings.	Ce sont des effets personnels.
I have a few small gifts for my friends.	J'ai quelques petits cadeaux pour mes amis.
I have 200 cigarettes, some wine and a bottle of spirits.	J'ai deux cent cigarettes, du vin et une bouteille de spiritueux.
They are for my personal consumption.	C'est pour mon usage personnel.
Do I have to pay duty?	Je dois payer des droits?
I have no other luggage.	Je n'ai pas d'autres bagages.
Do you want to see my handbag/briefcase?	Vous voulez voir mon sac/ma serviette?
I can't find my keys.	Je ne trouve pas mes clés.
I have 200 francs in currency and £100 in traveller's cheques.	J'ai deux cent francs en devises et cent livres en chèques de voyage.
I can't afford to pay duty.	Je n'ai pas d'argent pour payer les droits.
Can I leave it here in bond?	Puis-je l'entreposer ici?
Here is a list of the souvenirs I have bought.	Voilà une liste des souvenirs que j'ai achetés.
You haven't marked my suitcase.	Vous n'avez pas marqué ma valise.
May I leave now?	Je peux partir maintenant?

At Airports, Terminals and Stations

Where can I find a porter?	Où trouve-t-on un porteur?
a luggage trolley?	un chariot à bagages?
the left luggage office?	la consigne?
my registered luggage?	mes bagages enregistrés?
Have you seen the representative of my travel company?	Avez-vous vu le représentant de ma compagnie de voyages?
Take my bag to the bus/taxi/car.	Portez mon sac à l'autobus/ au taxi/à la voiture.
How much per case?	C'est combien par valise?

Toilets

Where is the ladies'/gentlemen's toilet?	Où sont les toilettes pour dames/pour messieurs?
Have you any soap?	Vous avez du savon?
toilet paper?	du papier hygiénique?
a clean towel?	une serviette propre?
a comb or hairbrush?	un peigne ou une brosse à cheveux?
Shall I leave a tip?	Je laisse un pourboire?

Telephone

Where are the public telephones?	Où y a-t-il des téléphones publics?
I need a telephone directory.	J'ai besoin d'un annuaire du téléphone.
Where can I get some change?	Où peut-on obtenir de la monnaie?

Can I dial this number or do I ask the operator?	**Puis-je téléphoner par l'automatique ou faut-il demander le standard?**
May I have Paris 1234.	**Donnez-moi le 12–34 (douze-trente-quatre) à Paris.**
Can I reverse the charges?	**Je voudrais téléphoner en P.C.V.**
I want a person-to-person call.	**Je voudrais une communication avec préavis.**
I have been cut off.	**On nous a coupés.**
You gave me the wrong number.	**Vous m'avez donné le mauvais numéro.**
Is she not in?	**Elle n'est pas là?**
Tell her I called. My name is ...	**Dites-lui que j'ai appelée. Je m'appelle ...**

Taxi Rank

Where can I get a taxi?	**Où est-ce qu'on trouve un taxi?**
Please get me a taxi.	**Pouvez-vous aller me chercher un taxi?**
Take me to St Cloud/this address.	**Conduisez-moi à Saint-Cloud/à cette adresse.**
How much will it cost?	**Ce sera combien?**
That's too much.	**C'est trop cher.**
Turn right/left at the next corner.	**Tournez à droite/à gauche au prochain coin.**
Go straight on.	**Allez tout droit.**

Airports, Terminals and Stations

I'll tell you when to stop.	**Je vous dirai quand vous arrêter.**
Stop!	**Arrêtez/Stop!**
I'm in a hurry.	**Je suis pressé.**
Take it easy.	**Ne vous en faites pas.**
Can you please carry my bags?	**Pouvez-vous porter mes bagages?**

Signs

Booking Office	**Guichet**
Cars Check-in Desk	**Contrôle des voitures**
Coach Station	**Gare routière**
Escalator	**Escalier roulant**
Exit	**Sortie**
Information Office	**Bureau de Renseignements**
Left Luggage	**Consigne**
Platform	**Quai**
Porters	**Porteurs**
Toilet	**Toilettes/W.C.**
Underground	**Métro**
Waiting Room	**Salle d'Attente**

Newsstand/Kiosk

Have you got an English paper or magazine?	**Avez-vous un journal ou un magazine anglais?**
Have you any paperbacks?	**Avez-vous des livres de poche?**

Which is the local paper?	**Quel est le journal local?**
Do you sell timetables?	**Vous vendez des indicateurs?**
Do you sell a guide/map of the city?	**Avez-vous un guide/un plan de la ville?**
Have you any writing paper and envelopes?	**Avez-vous du papier à lettres et des enveloppes?**
sellotape?	**du scotch?**
matches?	**des allumettes?**
stamps?	**des timbres?**
a ball-point pen?	**un stylo à bille?**
some string?	**de la ficelle?**

Information Bureau

Is there an information bureau here?	**Y a-t-il un Syndicat d'Initiative?**
Have you any leaflets?	**Avez-vous des dépliants?**
Have you a guide to the hotels?	**Avez-vous un guide des hôtels?**
pensions?	**des pensions?**
youth hostels?	**des auberges de jeunesse?**
camp sites?	**des terrains de camping?**
Do you find accommodation for visitors?	**Vous vous occupez de trouver des chambres?**
I want a first-class/second-class hotel.	**Je veux un hôtel quatre étoiles/trois étoiles.**
a pension.	**une pension.**
a double room.	**une chambre pour deux personnes.**
just a single room.	**simplement une chambre pour une personne.**

Airports, Terminals and Stations

We'll go right away.	**Nous y allons tout de suite.**
How do I get there?	**Quel chemin faut-il prendre pour y aller?**

At Airports

Where is the check-in desk?	**Où enregistre-t-on les bagages?**
Can I take this in the cabin?	**Je peux prendre ça dans la cabine?**
Do I have to pay excess?	**Faut-il payer un supplément?**
You haven't given me a luggage claim tag.	**Vous ne m'avez pas donné de reçu pour mes bagages.**
I've missed my flight. Can you give me another flight?	**J'ai manqué mon avion. Pouvez-vous me réserver une place dans un autre avion?**
Is there a bar on the other side of the customs barrier?	**Y a-t-il un bar de l'autre côté de la barrière douanière?**
Where is the flight indicator?	**Où est l'indicateur de vols?**
Is there a duty-free shop?	**Y a-t-il un magasin hors-taxe?**
Is there another way to go up/down other than by escalator?	**Y a-t-il un autre moyen de monter/de descendre que par l'escalier roulant?**
Where can I get some flight insurance?	**Où peut-on obtenir une assurance pour le voyage?**
Is there a wheelchair available?	**Auriez-vous une chaise d'invalide?**

Is the flight delayed?	**Est-ce que l'avion a du retard?**
At what time do we land?	**A quelle heure arriverons-nous?**

At Railway Stations

Where is the ticket office?	**Où sont les guichets?**
One single/return first-class/second-class ticket to ...	**Un billet simple/aller-retour de première/deuxième classe à ...**
How much is a child's fare?	**Combien coûte un billet pour enfants?**

Can I reserve a seat?
  a couchette?
  a sleeping berth?
	**Je peux réserver une place?
	  une couchette?
	  une place dans un wagon-lit?**

Is there a supplement to pay?	**Faut-il payer un supplément?**
Will there be a restaurant car/buffet car on the train?	**Est-ce qu'il y aura un wagon-restaurant/un buffet dans ce train?**
Do I have to change?	**Je dois changer?**
Which is the platform for the train to Biarritz?	**De quelle voie part le train de Biarritz?**
Does my friend need a platform ticket?	**Est-ce que mon ami a besoin d'un billet de quai?**
At what times does the train leave?	**A quelle heure part le train?**

At a Port

Which is quay number six?	**Quel est le quai numéro six?**
From where does the hovercraft leave?	**D'où part l'aéroglisseur?**
Where is the car ferry terminal?	**Où est le terminus du ferry?**
At what time can I go on board?	**A quelle heure peut-on monter à bord?**
Will there be an announcement when visitors must disembark?	**Est-ce qu'on préviendra les non-voyageurs quand il sera l'heure de quitter le bateau?**

VOCABULARY

bench	**le banc**
bus driver	**le conducteur d'autobus**
clock	**l'horloge**
gate	**la portière**
guard	**le chef de train**
left luggage office	**la consigne**
lockers	**la consigne automatique**
porter	**le porteur**
security officer	**l'agent de sécurité**
station buffet	**le buffet de la gare**
station master	**le chef de gare**
tannoy	**le haut-parleur**
ticket collector	**le contrôleur**
vending machine	**le distributeur automatique**
waiting room	**la salle d'attente**

En Route

General Expressions

At what time do we start/take off?	A quelle heure partons-nous?
Why is there a delay?	Pourquoi y a-t-il du retard?
Have I got time to go to the toilet?	Est-ce que j'ai le temps d'aller aux toilettes/W.C.?
I can't find my ticket.	Je ne trouve pas mon billet.
Take my address and passport number.	Prenez mon adresse et mon numéro de passeport.
Is this seat reserved?	Cette place est réservée?

Travelling by Air

Are you the Steward/Stewardess?	Etes-vous le Steward/Stewardess?
Which button do I press to call you?	Sur quel bouton faut-il appuyer pour vous appeler?
Can you help me to adjust my seat?	Pouvez-vous m'aider à ajuster mon siège?
Shall I fasten my seat belt?	Est-ce que je dois attacher ma ceinture de sécurité?
I haven't got a sick bag.	Je n'ai pas de sac en papier.
How high are we flying?	A quelle altitude sommes nous?
What town is that down there?	Quelle est cette ville, là en-bas?
Is there a map of the route?	Avez-vous une carte du parcours?

Travelling

Are there any duty-free goods available?	**Y a-t-il des marchandises hors-taxe?**
Can I pay you in foreign currency/in pounds sterling?	**Est-ce que je peux vous payer en devises étrangères/en livres sterling?**
The airvent is stuck.	**Le ventilateur est bloqué.**
May I change my seat?	**Puis-je changer de place?**

VOCABULARY

aircraft	**l'avion**
air terminal	**l'aérogare**
arrival gate	**la porte d'arrivée**
ashtray	**le cendrier**
flight deck	**le pont d'envol**
fuselage	**le fuselage**
jet engine	**le moteur à réaction**
light	**la lumière**
luggage shelf	**le compartiment à bagages**
propeller	**l'hélice**
tail	**la queue**
tray meal	**le repas**
window	**le hublot**
wing	**l'aîle**

SIGNS

Fasten your seat belts	**Attachez vos ceintures de sécurité**
Emergency exit	**Sortie de secours**
No smoking	**Défense de fumer**

Travelling by Motor Rail

I have booked my car by motor rail to Avignon.	**J'ai réservé une place pour ma voiture sur le train auto-couchettes d'Avignon.**
Does the ticket include insurance?	**Est-ce que l'assurance est comprise dans le prix du billet?**
At what time must I report?	**A quelle heure faut-il se présenter?**
Where is the loading platform?	**Où est la plate-forme de chargement?**
Shall I lock the car?	**Faut-il fermer la voiture à clé?**
Can I leave my belongings in the car?	**Est-ce que je peux laisser mes affaires dans la voiture?**
Where is our compartment?	**Où est notre compartiment?**
At what time do I have to drive off?	**A quelle heure dois-je débarquer?**

Travelling by Hovercraft

Which is the way to the hoverport?	**Quel est le chemin pour le hoverport?**
At what time can I drive on?	**Quand puis-je embarquer?**
Will there be access to the car deck during the crossing?	**Pourrai-je avoir accès à ma voiture pendant la traversée?**
Are refreshments served on board?	**Sert-on des rafraîchissements à bord?**
Is there a duty-free shop?	**Y a-t-il un magasin hors-taxe?**

Travelling

| Can I catch an earlier/later flight? | **Puis-je avancer/reculer mon départ?** |

Travelling by Rail

Where is carriage number five?	**Où est le wagon numéro cinq?**
I have a couchette reserved.	**J'ai réservé une couchette.**
This is my seat reservation.	**Voilà mon ticket de réservation.**
Is this seat taken?	**Cette place est prise?**
Is the dining car at the front or back?	**Est-ce que le wagon-restaurant est à l'avant ou à l'arrière?**
Two tickets for the first service please.	**Deux tickets pour le premier service, s'il vous plaît.**
Is the buffet car open throughout the journey?	**Est-ce que le buffet est ouvert pendant tout le voyage?**
Can I leave my big case in the baggage car?	**Est-ce que je peux mettre ma grande valise dans le fourgon?**
Is there an observation car?	**Y a-t-il une cabine d'observation?**
What station is this?	**A quelle gare sommes-nous?**
The heating is on/off. It is too high/too low.	**Le chauffage est allumé/éteint. Il fait trop chaud/pas assez chaud.**
I can't open/close the window.	**Je ne peux pas ouvrir/fermer cette fenêtre.**
Where do I have to change?	**Où est-ce que je change de train?**

Is this where I get my connection for Lyons?	**Est-ce que c'est ici que j'ai ma correspondance pour Lyon?**

VOCABULARY

blanket	**la couverture**
corridor	**le couloir**
compartment	**le compartiment**
cushion	**le coussin**
luggage rack	**le filet à bagages**
non-smoking	**pour non-fumeurs**
sleeping berth	**la couchette**
sleeping car	**le wagon-lit**
sliding door	**la porte à coulisse**

SIGNS

Do not lean out of the window.	**Ne pas se pencher par la fenêtre.**
Do not use the toilet while the train is stationary.	**Ne pas utiliser les toilettes/W.C. quand le train est en arrêt.**

Travelling on a Steamer

Where is the purser's office?	**Où est le bureau du commissaire?**
Please will you show me to my cabin?	**Pourriez-vous me conduire à ma cabine?**
Are you the steward?	**Etes-vous le steward?**

Travelling

Is there a children's nursery/ shop/gymnasium?	**Y a-t-il une crêche/une boutique/une salle de gymnastique?**
Where can I get some seasick tablets?	**Où trouve-t-on des cachets contre le mal de mer?**
On which side do we disembark?	**De quel côté débarquons-nous?**
The sea is calm/rough.	**La mer est calme/agitée.**
What are those birds? Seagulls?	**Quels sont ces oiseaux? Des mouettes?**
Is there a duty-free shop?	**Y a-t-il un magasin hors-taxe?**

Vocabulary

aft	à l'arrière
anchor	l'ancre
bridge	le pont
captain	le capitaine
crew	l'équipage
deck	le pont
funnel	la cheminée
lifebelt	la ceinture de sauvetage
lifeboat	le canot de sauvetage
mast	le mât
officer	l'officier
port (harbour)	le port
port (left)	à bâbord
radar	le radar
raft	le radeau
rail	le rail
starboard	à tribord

Danger – propellers   **Danger – hélices**

Travelling by Coach

Is this the coach for Orleans?	**C'est l'autocar pour Orléans?**
Can I sit near the driver?	**Je peux m'asseoir près du chauffeur?**
Are the seats numbered?	**Est-ce que les sièges sont numerotés?**
Do I pay on the coach?	**Est-ce qu'on paie dans l'autocar?**
How often does it stop?	**Combien de fois est-ce qu'il s'arrête?**
Would you mind closing the window? It's draughty.	**Pourriez-vous fermer la fenêtre? Il y a un courant d'air.**
Can you help me to carry my luggage?	**Pouvez-vous m'aider à porter mes bagages?**

VOCABULARY

back seat	**le siège arrière**
driver	**le chauffeur**
foot rest	**le repose-pied**
front seat	**le siège avant**
guide	**le guide**
luggage compartment	**le coffre**

Travelling

Buses and Metro

Where is the bus stop?	**Où est l'arrêt d'autobus?**
Does one have to queue?	**Faut-il faire la queue?**
Do I need a queue ticket?	**Est-ce qu'il me faut un numéro?**
Can I buy a book of tickets?	**Je peux acheter un carnet?**
Do you go by the Arc de Triomphe?	**Passez-vous près de l'Arc de Triomphe?**
Will you tell me when we reach the Champs Elysées?	**Pouvez-vous me dire quand on arrive aux Champs Elysées?**
I want to get off at the next stop.	**Je veux descendre au prochain arrêt.**
Will you ring the bell please?	**Pouvez-vous sonner?**
I want to go to the Bois de Boulogne.	**Je veux aller au Bois de Boulogne.**
Which line do I take?	**Quelle ligne faut-il prendre?**
Do I have to change?	**Je dois changer?**
At what time is the last metro?	**Quelle est l'heure du dernier métro?**
Here is a metro map. Press the button and your line lights up.	**Voilà un plan du métro. Poussez ce bouton et votre ligne s'allume.**

---

automatic door	**le portillon automatique**
barrier	**la barrière**

escalator   **l'escalier roulant**

S ɪ ɢ ɴ s
Reserved for war wounded   **Réservé aux blessés de guerre**

Other Vehicles

Where can I hire a bicycle?   **Où peut-on louer une bicyclette?**

  a moped?   **un vélomoteur?**
  a tricycle?   **un tricycle?**
  a tandem?   **un tandem?**

Please put some air in this tyre.   **Pourriez-vous gonfler ce pneu?**

One of the spokes is broken.   **Un des rayons est cassé.**

The brake is not working.   **Le frein ne marche pas.**

Do you have a bicycle with gears?   **Avez-vous une bicyclette avec changements de vitesse?**

The saddle needs lowering/raising.   **Il faut baisser/élever la selle.**

Are there any horse-drawn vehicles at this resort?   **Y a-t-il des charrettes à chevaux dans cette ville?**

Will you put the roof down, please?   **Pourriez-vous abaisser le toit?**

Will you take the children on the driver's box?   **Permettez-vous aux enfants de s'asseoir sur le siège du conducteur?**

Are the cable cars working?   **Est-ce que le funiculaire fonctionne?**

Is there a chair-lift?	**Y a-t-il un télésiège?**
Please adjust the safety bar for me.	**Pourriez-vous ajuster la barre de sécurité?**
Do they run frequently?	**Est-ce qu'ils circulent fréquemment?**
How high is the upper station?	**A quelle altitude se trouve l'arrêt du haut?**
Can I walk down?	**Est-ce que je peux descendre à pied?**
Do you sell season tickets?	**Vendez-vous des billets d'abonnement?**

VOCABULARY

bicycle pump	**la pompe à bicyclette**
carrier	**le porte-bagage**
chain	**la chaîne**
crossbar	**la barre**
donkey	**l'âne**
handlebars	**le guidon**
harness	**le harnais**
lamp	**le phare**
mudguard	**le garde-boue**
pedal	**la pédale**
rear light	**le feu arrière**
ski-lift	**le remonte-pente**
skis	**les skis**
sledge	**la luge**
toboggan	**le toboggan**
whip	**le fouet**

Walking About

IN TOWN

Is this the main shopping street?	**Est-ce que c'est la rue commerçante principale?**

Where is the town hall?
  police station?
  tourist office?
	**Où est l'hôtel de ville?
	  le commissariat de police?
	  le Syndicat d'Initiative?**

In what part of town are the theatres/nightclubs?	**Dans quel quartier se trouvent les théâtres/les clubs de nuit?**
Can I get there by bus/by underground/ on foot?	**On peut y aller en autobus/en métro/à pied?**
Where is the nearest station?	**Où est la gare la plus proche?**
Where is the nearest bus stop?	**Où est l'arrêt d'autobus le plus proche?**
Is there a market in the town?	**Y a-t-il un marché dans la ville?**
What day is market day?	**Quel est le jour de marché?**
Is the business centre near?	**Est-ce que le centre des affaires est près d'ici?**
Must one cross at the traffic lights?	**Est-ce qu'il faut traverser aux feux?**
Do pedestrians have right of way here?	**Est-ce que les piétons ont la priorité ici?**
Is there a public toilet near?	**Y a-t-il des toilettes publiques près d'ici?**

39

castle	**le château**
cathedral	**la cathédrale**
cemetery	**le cimetière**
church	**l'église**
city centre	**le centre de la ville**
concert hall	**la salle de concerts**
courts	**la cour de justice**
docks	**les docks**
exhibition	**l'exposition**
factory	**l'usine**
fortress	**la forteresse**
fountain	**la fontaine**
government buildings	**les bâtiments officiels**
gardens	**les jardins**
harbour	**le port**
lake	**le lac**
monastery	**le monastère**
monument	**le monument**
museum	**le musée**
old town	**la vieille ville**
opera house	**l'Opéra**
palace	**le palais**
park	**le parc/le jardin public**
ruins	**les ruines**
shopping centre	**le centre commercial**
stadium	**le stade**
statue	**la statue**
stock exchange	**la Bourse**
subway	**le métro**
traffic lights	**les feux de signalisation**
tower	**la tour**
university	**l'université**
zoo	**le zoo**

IN THE COUNTRY

May we walk through here?	**On peut passer par là?**
Is this a public footpath?	**C'est un sentier public?**
Do I need permission to fish?	**Faut-il obtenir la permission de pêcher?**
Which way is north/south/east/west?	**Où est le nord/le sud/l'est/l'ouest?**
Is there a bridge or ford across this stream?	**Y a-t-il un pont, ou un passage à gué, sur cette rivière?**
How far is the nearest village?	**A quelle distance se trouve le village le plus proche?**
I am lost. Can you please direct me to ...?	**Je suis égaré. Pouvez-vous m'indiquer la direction de ...?**
Will you please show me the route on this map?	**Pouvez-vous me montrer la route à suivre sur cette carte?**

VOCABULARY

barn	**la grange**
bird	**l'oiseau**
brook	**le ruisseau**
canal	**le canal**
cliff	**la falaise**
cottage	**la petite maison de campagne**
cow	**la vache**
dog	**le chien**
farm	**la ferme**
field	**le champ**
footpath	**le sentier**

forest	**la forêt**
heath	**la lande**
hill	**la colline**
horse	**le cheval**
goat	**la chèvre**
inn	**l'auberge**
lake	**le lac**
marsh	**le marécage**
moorland	**la lande**
mountain	**la montagne**
orchard	**le verger**
peak	**le sommet**
pond	**la mare**
river	**la rivière**
sea	**la mer**
sheep	**le mouton**
spring	**la source**
stream	**le cours d'eau**
swamp	**le marais**
tree	**l'arbre**
valley	**la vallée**
village	**le village**
vineyard	**la vigne**
waterfall	**la cascade**
well	**le puits**
wood	**le bois**

Motoring

At the Frontier

Here is my registration book.	**Voilà mon carnet de route.**
green card insurance.	**ma carte d'assurance internationale.**
driving licence.	**mon permis de conduire.**
I have an international licence.	**J'ai un permis international.**

This is a translation of my British licence.	**Voilà une traduction de mon permis britannique.**
This is a self-drive car. Here are the documents.	**C'est une voiture de location. Voilà les documents.**
Do you want to open the boot?	**Voulez-vous ouvrir le coffre?**
I arrived today.	**Je suis arrivé aujourd'hui.**
I am staying for two weeks.	**Je reste pendant deux semaines.**
We are passing through on the way to Italy.	**Nous sommes de passage; nous allons en Italie.**
Does this customs post close at night?	**Est-ce que ce poste de douane ferme la nuit?**
At what time?	**A quelle heure?**
Shall I leave my engine running?	**Est-ce que je dois laisser le moteur en marche?**
Do you want me to stop the engine?	**Voulez-vous que j'arrête le moteur?**

On the Road

French roads are classified as follows:

Autoroute	**A**
Route Nationale	**N**
Route départementale	**D**
Chemin communal	**C**
Chemin rural	**R**

Autoroutes are excellent but you have to pay to drive on them, which can be quite expensive. On the autoroutes there are good service areas and excellent restaurants. National and

departmental roads go through towns and villages which you
would miss on the autoroute. Country roads are narrow and
picturesque – perfect if you are not in a hurry and want to
absorb the atmosphere of the region through which you are
travelling.

Can you tell me the way to Autun?	**La route pour Autun, s'il vous plaît?**
How many kilometres is it?	**C'est à combien de kilomètres?**
Is it a good road?	**C'est une bonne route?**
It is hilly/flat/straight/winding?	**Est-ce qu'elle est accidentée/ plate/droite/en lacets?**
What is the speed limit on this section?	**Quelle est la limite de vitesse ici?**
Will you point out the route on this map please?	**Voulez-vous m'indiquer la route sur cette carte?**
How much does this section of motorway cost?	**Combien faut-il payer pour cette section d'autoroute?**
Do I pay at the exit?	**Est-ce que je paie à la sortie?**
I am sorry, I have no change.	**Excusez-moi mais je n'ai pas de monnaie.**
How far is it to the next petrol station?	**Où se trouve la station service la plus proche?**
I want twenty five litres, please.	**Donnez-moi vingt-cinq litres, s'il vous plaît.**
Give me twenty francs' worth.	**Donnez-m'en pour vingt francs.**
Fill her up, please.	**Faites le plein, s'il vous plaît.**
Please check the oil and water.	**Voulez-vous vérifier l'huile et l'eau?**

I need some air in the tyres.	**Mes pneus ont besoin d'être pompés.**
I think the windscreen fluid needs topping up.	**Je crois qu'il faut ajouter du liquide pour le pare-brise.**
Have you any distilled water for the battery?	**Avez-vous de l'eau distillée pour la batterie?**
Please clean the windscreen.	**Pourriez-vous nettoyer le pare-brise?**
Have you any paper towels?	**Avez-vous des serviettes de papier?**
Have you got a car wash?	**Avez-vous un service de lavage des voitures?**
Do you sell yellow filters for the headlights?	**Avez-vous des filtres jaunes pour les phares?**
Can I park here?	**Je peux stationner ici?**
Where is the nearest car park?	**Où est le parking le plus proche?**

Trouble with the Police

Usually the police are polite and helpful to visitors, but they are more likely to be so if you appear friendly and co-operative. A few phrases in their language can sometimes work miracles.

I'm sorry, I did not see you signal.	**Excusez-moi, mais je n'ai pas vu votre signal.**
I thought I had right of way.	**Je croyais avoir la priorité.**
I apologize. I won't do it again.	**Je vous demande pardon. Cela n'arrivera plus.**
Here is my name and address.	**Voilà mon nom et mon adresse.**

Motoring

This is my passport.	**Voilà mon passeport.**
Do I have to pay a fine?	**Est-ce que je dois payer une amende?**
How much?	**Combien?**
I haven't got any cash on me. Can I settle up at the police station?	**Je n'ai pas d'argent sur moi. Est-ce que je peux régler cela au commissariat de police?**
Thank you for your courtesy.	**Je vous remercie de votre amabilité.**

Car Rental

I want to hire a small car.	**Je voudrais louer une petite voiture.**
a family saloon.	**une berline.**
a large car.	**une grande voiture.**
a sports car.	**une voiture de sport.**
a van.	**une camionnette.**
I shall need it for ten days.	**Il me la faudra pour dix jours.**
How much is the daily charge?	**Quel est le prix de location par jour?**
Is it cheaper by the week?	**Est-ce que c'est moins cher en payant à la semaine?**
Does that include mileage and insurance?	**Est-ce que le kilométrage et l'assurance sont inclus?**
What is the mileage charge?	**Que faut-il payer pour le kilométrage?**
Does the insurance cover the car and the passengers?	**Est-ce que la voiture et les passagers sont couverts par l'assurance?**

Where do I pick up the car?	**Où est-ce que je vais chercher la voiture?**
Can you bring it to my hotel?	**Pouvez-vous me l'amener à l'hôtel?**
Can I leave it at another town or at the airport?	**Est-ce que je peux la laisser dans une autre ville ou à l'aéroport?**
Is there a deposit to pay?	**Faut-il payer un acompte?**
May I pay with my credit card?	**Est-ce que je peux payer avec ma carte de crédit?**
Will you please check the documents with me?	**Pourriez-vous vérifier les documents avec moi?**
Will you show me the gears and the instrument panel?	**Pouvez-vous me montrer les vitesses et le tableau de bord?**
Is the tank full?	**Est-ce que le réservoir est plein?**

Road Signs

Allumez vos phares	Switch on your headlights
Attention travaux	Roadworks ahead
Chaussée déformée	Damaged road surface
Chute de pierres	Falling stones
Douane	Customs
Fin de l'interdiction de doubler	End of no overtaking
Interdiction de doubler	No overtaking
Interdit aux piétons/aux poids lourds	No pedestrians/no heavy vehicles

Interdiction de stationner	No parking
Nids de poules	Pot holes
Passage à niveau	Level crossing
Passage protégé	Priority for vehicles on main road
Priorité à droite	Priority for vehicles coming from the right
Réservé aux piétons	Pedestrians only
Déviation	Diversion
Route étroite/glissante	Narrow/slippery road
Sens interdit	No entry
Serrez à droite	Keep to the right
Sortie des camions	Lorries turning
Stationnement autorisé/ interdit	Parking permitted/ prohibited
Verglas	Black ice
Virage sur 3 km	Bends for 3 kilometres
Zone bleue	Parking meter zone

Trouble on the Road

OTHER PEOPLE'S

There has been an accident three miles back.	**Il y a eu un accident à cinq kilomètres d'ici.**
Will you phone the police, please?	**Pourriez-vous téléphoner à la police?**
No, I did not see it happen.	**Non, je n'ai pas vu l'accident.**

The car's registration number was ...	**Le numéro d'immatriculation de la voiture était ...**
I do not think anyone is hurt.	**Je ne crois pas que quelqu'un soit blessé.**
Someone is badly hurt.	**Il y a un blessé grave.**

Yours

Are you all right?	**Ça va?**
My passengers are not hurt.	**Mes passagers ne sont pas blessés.**
The car is damaged.	**La voiture est endommagée.**
May I have your insurance details?	**Pouvez-vous me donner des détails sur votre assurance?**
Your name and address, please?	**Votre nom et votre adresse, s'il vous plaît.**
Will you please fill out this form?	**Pouvez-vous remplir ce formulaire?**
I think we shall have to call the police.	**Je crois qu'il faudra appeler la police.**
Excuse me, would you mind being a witness?	**Pardon, est-ce que vous voulez bien être témoin?**
It happened because he braked suddenly.	**C'est arrivé parce qu'il a freiné brusquement.**
He came out of a side road without signalling.	**Il sortait d'une route latérale sans avertir.**
He tried to overtake on a narrow stretch of road.	**Il a essayé de doubler à un endroit où la route est étroite.**
He turned off without signalling.	**Il a tourné sans prévenir.**

49

May I explain to someone who understands English?	**Est-ce que je peux expliquer à quelqu'un qui comprend l'anglais?**

If you are unfortunate enough to have an accident, be sure to get all the details from the other driver involved. Your insurance company will have provided you with an accident report form. Fill it up on the spot with the help of the other driver. Above all, keep cool.

Breakdown

If you have a breakdown put the red triangle behind your car at once or you may be penalized. Get the car off the road if possible.

Thank you for stopping. I am in trouble.	**Merci de vous être arrêté. Je suis en difficulté.**
Will you help me?	**Voulez-vous m'aider?**
My car has broken down.	**Ma voiture est en panne.**
Will you tell the next garage or breakdown service vehicles that you pass?	**Pouvez-vous prévenir le premier garage que vous verrez ou le service de dépannage?**
Will you please telephone a garage for me?	**Pourriez-vous téléphoner à un garage à ma place?**
Can you give me a lift to the next telephone?	**Pourriez-vous m'emmener au téléphone le plus proche?**
Can you send a breakdown truck?	**Pourriez-vous faire venir un camion de dépannage?**
I am three kilometres from Chartres on the N ...	**Je suis à trois kilomètres de Chartres sur la N ...**
How long will you be?	**Dans combien de temps viendrez-vous?**

Repairs

There's something wrong with the engine.	**Il y a quelque chose qui ne va pas dans le moteur.**
The clutch is slipping.	**L'embrayage patine.**
There is a noise from the . . .	**Il y a un bruit qui vient de . . .**
The brakes are not working.	**Les freins ne marchent pas.**
The water system is leaking.	**Il y a une fuite dans le système d'eau.**
My fan belt is broken.	**La courroie du ventilateur est cassée.**
I've got a flat tyre.	**J'ai un pneu crevé.**
The electrical system has failed.	**Le système électrique ne marche pas.**
The engine is overheating.	**Le moteur chauffe trop.**
The car won't start.	**La voiture ne démarre pas.**
What is the matter?	**Qu'est-ce qui ne va pas?**
Is it broken?	**C'est cassé?**
burnt out?	**brûlé?**
disconnected?	**débranché?**
jammed?	**bloqué?**
Is it leaking?	**Ça fuit?**
Is there a short circuit?	**Y a-t-il un court-circuit?**
Do I need a new part?	**Me faut-il une pièce de rechange?**
Is there a Ford agent in town?	**Y a-t-il un agent Ford en ville?**
Can you send for the part?	**Pouvez-vous obtenir la pièce de rechange?**

51

Motoring

Is it serious?	**C'est grave?**
How long will it take to repair?	**Combien de temps vous faudra-t-il pour faire la réparation?**
Can I hire another car?	**Est-ce que je peux louer une autre voiture?**
What will it cost?	**Ce sera combien?**
I will get the part flown from Britain.	**Je ferai venir la pièce d'Angleterre par avion.**
Your mechanic has been very kind. I would like to tip him.	**Votre mécanicien a été très obligeant. Je voudrais lui donner un pourboire.**

VOCABULARY

battery	**la batterie**
brakes	**les freins**
brake lining	**la garniture de freins**
bulbs	**les ampoules**
carburettor	**le carburateur**
clutch	**l'embrayage**
cooling system	**le système de refroidissement**
dip stick	**la jauge d'huile**
dynamo	**la dynamo**
distributor	**le distributeur**
electrical system	**le système électrique**
engine	**le moteur**
exhaust pipe	**le tuyau d'échappement**
fan	**le ventilateur**
filter	**le filtre**
fuel pump	**la pompe d'alimentation**
fuel tank	**le réservoir**
gears	**les vitesses**

generator	la dynamo
hand brake	le frein à main
headlights	les phares
heating system	le chauffage
horn	le claxon
ignition	l'allumage
indicator	l'indicateur
lubrication system	le système de lubrification
radiator	le radiateur
reflector	le réflecteur
seat	le siège
silencer	le pot d'échappement
sparking plug	la bougie
speedometer	le compteur
suspension	la suspension
transmission	la transmission
wheels	les roues
windscreen wipers	les essuie-glaces

A Place to Stay

There are places to suit every budget level in French-speaking Europe from the great luxury palaces of the Riviera to the **brasserie** with rooms to let. If you have not booked a hotel in advance, ask at the **Syndicat d'Initiative** in each town. They will help you find a place within your price range. If you don't want to stay at a hotel there are **pensions**, rooms in private houses, apartments and country cottages (called **gîtes** in France) and, of course, camping sites. The standards of comfort vary considerably and one must remember that the French value a good meal above a good mattress, or even good plumbing.

Hotels and Pensions

Finding a Room

I am travelling with the . . . travel agency.	**Je voyage avec l'agence de voyage . . .**
Here is my hotel coupon.	**Voilà mon ticket pour l'hôtel.**
My room is already reserved.	**Ma chambre est déjà réservée.**
I am travelling independently.	**Je voyage indépendamment.**
Will a porter bring my luggage in?	**Est-ce qu'un porteur peut m'apporter mes bagages?**
Can I leave my car here?	**Est-ce que je peux laisser ma voiture ici?**
Is there a car park?	**Y a-t-il un parking?**
Are you the receptionist/ concierge/manager?	**Etes vous la réceptionniste/le concierge/le gérant?**

Have you a single/double/three-bedded room?	Avez-vous une chambre pour une personne/deux personnes/à trois lits?
with a bath and separate toilet?	avec une baignoire et des toilettes séparées?
with bath or shower?	avec une baignoire ou une douche?
with a balcony?	avec un balcon?
looking over the front/back?	donnant sur le devant/l'arrière?
How much is it per day?	C'est combien par jour?
Is there a reduction for a longer stay/for children?	Y a-t-il une réduction pour un séjour prolongé/pour les enfants?
Are there special mealtimes for children?	Est-ce que les enfants mangent à des heures différentes?
I don't want to pay more than ... francs per day.	Je ne veux pas payer plus de ... francs par jour.
Have you anything cheaper?	Avez-vous quelque chose de meilleur marché?
Do I have to fill in a visitor's card?	Faut-il remplir une fiche?
Here is my passport.	Voilà mon passeport.
How long will you keep it?	Combien de temps le garderez-vous?
I'd like to go up to my room right away.	Je voudrais monter à ma chambre tout-de-suite.
Will you send up the luggage?	Pourriez-vous faire monter mes bagages?

Accommodation

This case is for room 3 and that one for number 12.	**Cette valise va dans la chambre trois, celle-ci est pour le numéro douze.**
May I have the room key?	**Pouvez-vous me donner ma clé?**
Is the key in the door?	**Est-ce que la clé est sur la porte?**
Where is the lift?	**Où est l'ascenseur?**
Do I work it myself?	**Est-ce que je peux le faire fonctionner?**
Do you do breakfast?	**Servez-vous le petit-déjeuner?**
Do you do demi-pension?	**Faites-vous demi-pension?**
Can I put all extras on my bill?	**Est-ce que toutes mes dépenses supplémentaires peuvent être portées sur ma note?**
Is there a post box in the hotel?	**Y a-t-il une boîte aux lettres dans l'hôtel?**
Can you get the daily papers for me?	**Pouvez-vous me procurer les journaux quotidiens?**

Moving In

This room is too small/large/noisy/dark/high up.	**Cette chambre est trop petite/grande/bruyante/sombre/à un étage trop élevé.**
You haven't got a double bed?	**N'avez-vous pas un lit pour deux personnes?**

56

Please make the twin beds into one double.	**Pouvez-vous pousser ces deux lits pour en faire un grand?**
I need a child's cot.	**Il me faut un lit d'enfant.**
I shall need another pillow/ blanket.	**Il me faudrait encore un oreiller/une couverture.**
some clothes hangers.	**des cintres.**
some writing paper.	**du papier à lettre.**
The bedside light is not working.	**La lampe de chevet ne marche pas.**
The bulb is broken.	**L'ampoule est cassée.**
Which is the hot/cold tap?	**Quel est le robinet d'eau chaude/froide?**
Is this the electric razor socket?	**C'est la prise pour rasoirs électriques?**
What is the voltage?	**Quel est le voltage?**
My plug doesn't fit.	**Ma prise ne convient pas.**
Have you got an adaptor?	**Avez-vous un raccord?**
Is there an electrician in the village?	**Y a-t-il un électricien au village?**
Is there a hotel laundry?	**Y a-t-il un service de blanchisserie à l'hôtel?**
Are there facilities for washing and ironing clothes?	**Y a-t-il la possibilité de laver et de repasser?**
The blind is stuck.	**Le store est coincé.**
Will you bring me a bottle of drinking water?	**Pourriez-vous m'apporter une bouteille d'eau potable?**
Can I leave valuables in the hotel safe?	**Est-ce que je peux laisser mes objets de valeur dans le coffre-fort de l'hôtel?**

Accommodation

What time is breakfast/lunch/ dinner?	**A quelle heure est le petit- déjeuner/le déjeuner/le dîner?**
Do you serve breakfast in bed?	**Servez-vous le petit- déjeuner dans la chambre?**
Does the hotel do packed lunches?	**Est-ce que l'hôtel prépare des déjeuners à emporter?**

Small Hotels and Pensions

Do you have set times for meals?	**Est-ce que les repas sont à heures fixes?**
May I have a towel and soap?	**Je voudrais une serviette et du savon.**
At what time do you lock the front door at night?	**A quelle heure fermez-vous la porte d'entrée le soir?**
May I have a key?	**Pouvez-vous me donner une clé?**
Is it all right to leave the car in the street?	**Est-ce qu'on peut laisser la voiture dans la rue?**
Will our things be safe?	**Est-ce que nos affaires seront en sécurité?**
Where is the nearest garage?	**Où est le garage le plus proche?**

Rooms in Private Houses

Do you have a room free?	**Avez-vous une chambre libre?**
You don't do breakfast?	**Vous ne servez pas le petit- déjeuner?**
Is there a café nearby?	**Y a-t-il un café près d'ici?**

Would you like me to pay now?	**Voulez-vous que je paie maintenant?**
At what time will it be convenient to use the bathroom?	**A quelle heure est-ce que je pourrai utiliser la salle de bain?**
Do I need to tell you if I have a bath?	**Est-ce qu'il faut vous prévenir quand on prend un bain?**
Could you wake us in the morning?	**Pourriez-vous nous réveiller demain matin?**
Is there a lounge?	**Y a-t-il un salon?**
Shall I lock my room?	**Est-ce que je dois fermer ma porte à clé?**

Paying the Bill

May I have my bill please?	**Ma note, s'il vous plaît.**
Will you prepare my bill for first thing tomorrow?	**Pouvez-vous préparer ma note pour demain matin de bonne heure?**
I think there is a mistake.	**Je crois qu'il y a une erreur.**
I don't understand this item.	**Je ne comprends pas ce détail.**
May I pay by cheque?	**Vous prenez un chèque?**
Yes, I have a Eurocheque card.	**Oui, j'ai une carte Eurochèque.**
Do you accept credit cards?	**Vous acceptez les cartes de crédit?**
Is service included?	**Le service est compris?**
Is VAT included?	**La TVA est comprise?**

Accommodation

I would like a receipt, please.	**Je voudrais un reçu s'il vous plaît.**
Please forward my mail to . . .	**Pouvez-vous faire suivre mon courrier à . . .**
We have enjoyed ourselves very much.	**Nous nous sommes bien plus.**
May I have one of your leaflets?	**Est-ce que je peux avoir une de vos feuilles publicitaires?**

VOCABULARY

bar	**le bar**
barman	**le barman**
bed	**le lit**
chair	**la chaise**
chambermaid	**la femme de chambre**
children's playground	**le terrain de récréation**
discotheque	**la discothèque**
door	**la porte**
hall	**l'entrée**
lift	**l'ascenseur**
lounge	**le salon**
light switch	**l'interrupteur**
luggage porter	**le porteur**
manager	**le gérant**
mirror	**la glace**
night club	**la boîte de nuit**
playroom	**la salle de jeux**
radio	**la radio**
restaurant	**le restaurant**
stairs	**l'escalier**
swimming pool	**la piscine**
telephone operator	**la standardiste**
waiter	**le garçon**

waitress	la serveuse
wardrobe	l'armoire
window	la fenêtre

Catering for Yourself

Villas and Apartments

I have booked a villa/apartment.	J'ai loué une villa/un appartement.
Here is my voucher.	Voici ma fiche.
Will you please show me around?	Pouvez-vous me faire visiter?
Where is the light switch/power point/fuse box?	Où est l'interrupteur/la prise de courant/la boîte à fusibles?
Do all the outside doors lock?	Est-ce que toutes les portes extérieures ferment à clé?
How do the shutters work?	Comment est-ce que les volets fonctionnent?
Will you show me the hot water system?	Pouvez-vous me faire voir le système d'eau chaude?
Where is the mains valve?	Où est le robinet d'arrêt?
Is there mains gas?	Y a-t-il le gaz de ville?
Are gas cylinders delivered?	Est-ce que les bouteilles de gaz sont livrées à domicile?
At what time does the house help come?	A quelle heure la femme de ménage vient-elle?
Can we have three sets of house keys?	Pouvez-vous nous donner trois trousseaux de clés de la maison?

Catering for Yourself

When is the rubbish collected?	**Quand est-ce qu'on vide les poubelles?**
Are the shops near by?	**Y a-t-il des magasins près d'ici?**
Where is the bus stop/station?	**Où est l'arrêt d'autobus/la gare?**
Have you a map of the resort?	**Avez-vous un plan de la ville?**

Camping

Have you a site free?	**Avez-vous un emplacement libre?**
Do you rent out bungalows? tents? cooking equipment?	**Louez-vous des bungalows? des tentes? le matériel de cuisine?**
Are there toilet and washing facilities? cooking facilities?	**Y a-t-il des sanitaires?** **un endroit pour faire la cuisine?**
How much does it cost per night?	**C'est combien par nuit?**
Can I put my tent here?	**Est-ce que je peux monter ma tente ici?**
Is there room for a trailer?	**Y a-t-il de la place pour une remorque?**
Is there a night guard?	**Y a-t-il un gardien de nuit?**
Where is the camp shop? the restaurant? the nearest shopping centre?	**Où est le magasin du camp? le restaurant? le centre commercial le plus proche?**

At what time do we have to vacate the site?	**A quelle heure faut-il quitter l'emplacement?**
Where is the drinking tap?	**Où est l'eau potable?**

VOCABULARY

barbecue	**une barbecue**
basin	**une cuvette**
bucket	**un seau**
camping gas	**du gaz butane**
grill	**un gril**
guy ropes	**des tendeurs**
ice bucket	**une glacière**
insecticide	**un insecticide**
knife	**un couteau**
mosquito repellent	**de la crème contre les moustiques**
penknife	**un canif**
sleeping bag	**un sac de couchage**
spade	**une bêche**
stove	**un réchaud**
tent	**une tente**
tent peg	**un piquet**
waterproof sheet	**un tapis isolant**

Youth Hostelling

Is there a youth hostel in this town?	**Y a-t-il une auberge de jeunesse dans cette ville?**
Have you room for tonight?	**Avez-vous de la place pour ce soir?**

Catering for Yourself

We are members of the Youth Hostels Association.	**Nous sommes membres de l'Association des Auberges de Jeunesse.**
What are the house rules?	**Quel est le règlement?**
How long can we stay?	**Combien de jours pouvons nous rester?**
Is there a youth hostel at . . . ?	**Y a-t-il une auberge de jeunesse à . . . ?**

Eating and Drinking

Meal times not only offer a chance to satisfy the appetite, but they also provide an intimate glimpse of the life of the places you are visiting. Regional specialities reveal something of the character of the local environment. How different, for example, are the dishes of Normandy and Brittany to those of Provence. In the former, the farms and apple orchards contribute creamy sauces, rich cheeses, ciders, apple juices and Calvados. In Provence olive oil and the aromatic herbs of the warm south enrich the dishes of Mediterranean fish.

Above all, meal times provide an opportunity to watch the fascinating drama of people: the farmers at the village **brasserie**, the families at Sunday lunch, the fishermen at the quayside **bistro**. Different types of restaurant satisfy different tastes and there is a wide variety.

An **auberge** is an inn and a **bistro** is a small and informal tavern restaurant. A **brasserie** is larger and provides a café, bar and meal service. **Cafés** serve beer and coffee with a snack service. **Hôtelleries** are found in the country and are usually of the coaching inn style. A **relais de campagne** is a country inn. Restaurants are of various categories, from one-man shows to sophisticated four-star establishments. Restaurants that specialize in grills are often called **rôtisseries**. To those who travel by car, the **relais routiers** have become synonymous with good and inexpensive food. Originally they were patronized by truck drivers and other professional road users, and the presence of trucks and lorries outside them is always a good recommendation.

Can you recommend a good restaurant?	**Pouvez-vous me recommander un bon restaurant?**
not too expensive?	**pas trop cher?**
typical of the region?	**typique de la région?**
where there is music?	**où il y a de la musique?**

a four-star establishment?	**un restaurant quatre étoiles?**
a Chinese/Indian/Arab/Italian/Provençal/Normandy/Parisian restaurant?	**un restaurant chinois/indien/arabe/italien/provençal/normand/parisien?**
Is there a good snack bar nearby?	**Y a-t-il un bon snack-bar près d'ici?**
Where can I find a self-service restaurant?	**Où y a-t-il un restaurant self-service?**
Do I need to reserve a table?	**Est-ce qu'il faut réserver une table?**
I'd like a table for two at nine o'clock, please.	**Je voudrais une table pour deux à neuf heures, s'il vous plaît.**
not too near the door. in the corner. away from the kitchen.	**pas trop près de la porte. dans le coin. pas à proximité de la cuisine.**

At the Restaurant

A greeting often used in provincial towns and villages on entering a restaurant.	**Messieurs, Dames.**
A table for four, please.	**Une table pour quatre personnes, s'il vous plaît.**
Is this our table?	**C'est notre table?**
This table will do fine.	**Cette table nous conviendra très bien.**
The tablecloth is dirty.	**La nappe est sale.**

The table is unsteady.	**La table est bancale.**
The ashtray is missing.	**Il n'y a pas de cendrier.**
May I see the menu?	**Le menu, s'il vous plaît.**
We will have an aperitif while we look at it.	**Nous prendrons un apéritif pendant que nous faisons notre choix.**
Please bring the wine list.	**La carte des vins s'il vous plaît.**
Have you a set menu?	**Avez-vous un menu du jour?**
What do you recommend today?	**Qu'est-ce que vous recommandez aujourd'hui?**
What does it consist of?	**Quelle en est la composition?**
It sounds good. I'll try it.	**Ça me paraît bon. Je vais essayer.**
The soup is cold. Please warm it up.	**La soupe est froide. Pouvez-vous la réchauffer?**
This fork is dirty. May I have a clean one?	**Cette fourchette est sale. Pouvez-vous m'en donner une propre?**
Will you call our waiter?	**Pouvez-vous appeler notre garçon?**
We did not order this.	**Nous n'avons pas commandé ça.**
I'd like to speak to the head waiter.	**Je voudrais parler au maître d'hôtel.**
My compliments to the chef.	**Mes compliments au chef de cuisine.**
It's very good.	**C'est très bon.**
Have you any house wine?	**Avez-vous du vin de la maison (du patron)?**

Eating and Drinking

I'd like a half bottle/a carafe.	**Je voudrais une demi bouteille/une carafe.**
Which is the local wine?	**Quel est le vin local?**
This wine is corked.	**Ce vin sent le bouchon.**
The children will share a portion.	**Les enfants pourront se partager une part.**
May we have some water?	**Vous voulez bien nous apporter de l'eau?**
Have you any mineral water?	**Avez-vous de l'eau minerale?**
Have you a high chair for the child?	**Avez-vous une chaise haute pour cet enfant?**
Please bring some cushions.	**Pouvez-vous apporter des coussins?**
Where are the toilets?	**Où sont les toilettes?**

The Menu

Menus will vary from place to place. Most restaurants display them outside and they offer set meals from a simple menu for tourists to the **menu gastronomique** for the gourmet. There is usually a cover charge of ten to fifteen per cent, and V.A.T. is also added. The French reputation for excellent food is well earned and, at whatever level you choose to eat, you can usually count on a good meal. '**Bon appetit**', as the French say to each other when beginning a meal.

Starters

assiette anglaise	cold meats
asperges	asparagus

avocado	avocado
charcuterie assortie	variety of smoked sausages
crudités	slivers of raw vegetables
hors d'oeuvres	hors d'oeuvres
jambon	ham
jambonneau	ham knuckle
oeuf mayonnaise	egg mayonnaise
tapenade	boiled eggs with yolk mixed with anchovies
pâté	pâté
quiche	quiche
moules marinières farcies	stuffed mussels in wine
quenelles de brochet	pike balls
terrine	a kind of pâté
tête de veau	calf's head
saumon fumé	smoked salmon
huîtres	oysters
fruits de mer	seafood (shellfish)

Soups

aigo bouido	garlic soup
bisque de homard, d'écrevisses	lobster or shrimp soup
bouillabaisse	a rich stew of Mediterranean fish
bouillon	broth
consommé	consommé

crème de ...	cream of ...
julienne	clear soup with vegetables
potage de ...	thick soup
soupe	soup (usually with whole pieces of ingredients)
velouté de ...	same as cream of ...

Fish

anchoiade	anchovy pâté
bourride	fish stew
brandade de morue	creamed dried cod
crevettes	shrimps
coquilles St Jacques	scallops
dartois de sardines	sardines in a pastry case
écrevisses à la bordelaise	shrimps in wine sauce
filets de sole bonne femme	sole with wine and mushrooms
bercy	with red wine, mushrooms and onions
dieppoise	with mussels
marie waleska	with shrimps
meunière	with butter
mantua	with white sauce and crayfish
normande	with cream sauce
homard à l'armoricaine	lobster with butter, tomatoes and onion sauce
turbot au beurre blanc	turbot with butter sauce
saumon fumé	smoked salmon
matelote	fish stew

mousse de saumon	salmon mousse
truite en papillotte	trout baked in a paper bag
quenelles de brochet	pike forcemeat balls
poisson grillé/au four/ marine/poché/à la vapeur	fish grilled/in the oven/ marinated/poached/steamed

Meat

blanquette de veau	a white ragout of veal
boeuf en chemise	beef in pastry
boeuf stroganoff	beef slivers in cream and paprika
boeuf bourguignon	beef stewed in wine
biftecks (bien cuit, à point, saignant)	steak (well done, medium, rare)
carbonnade	beef stewed with vegetables
châteaubriant	large fillet steak
carré de porc	loin of pork
carré d'agneau	loin of lamb
cassoulet toulousain	lamb and bean stew
cochon de lait	sucking pig
ragoût	casserole/stew
choucroute garnie	sauerkraut with sausages, ham etc.
côte de porc	pork chop
cervelles au beurre noir	brains in black butter sauce
escaloppe de veau	veal escalope
estouffade de boeuf	slowly stewed beef

entrecôte	entrecote steak
foie à la moutarde	liver with mustard sauce
gigot d'agneau	leg of lamb
daube de mouton	braised mutton
épaule d'agneau	shoulder of lamb
queue de boeuf	oxtail
médaillons de boeuf	tournedos
paupiettes de veau	thin slices of veal stuffed with forcemeat
selle d'agneau	saddle of lamb
rognons de boeuf à la charentaise	kidneys, Charentaise style
tripe à la mode de Caen	tripe, Caen style

Sauces and Styles of Cooking

aïoli	a mayonnaise with strong garlic flavour
américaine	tomatoes, white wine, garlic and herbs
béarnaise	a creamy egg-yolk sauce flavoured with shallots and tarragon
béchamel	white sauce
beurre, blanc or noir	butter sauce flavoured with wine or vinegar (browned in the latter case)
bigarade	brown sauce with oranges
bordelaise	beef marrow, mushrooms, shallots and wine

bourguignonne	wine and herbs
café de Paris	brandy, herbs and butter
catalane	tomatoes, garlic and orange
chasseur	mushrooms, onions, shallots, peppers and wine
chaud-froid	a cold jelly dressing
diable	hot peppers
duxelles	mushrooms
financière	madeira, truffles, olives, mushrooms
forestière	mushrooms
hollandaise	egg yolks and lemon juice
lyonnaise	white sauce with onions
madère	madeira wine
maître d'hôtel	garnish with butter and parsley
marchand de vin	red wine and shallots
marinière	white wine, onions and egg yolks
meunière	butter, parsley, lemon juice
mornay	white cheese sauce
mousseline	mayonnaise with cream
périgourdine	truffles
normande	mushrooms, eggs and cream
poivrade	pepper sauce
provençale	tomatoes, onions, garlic
remoulade	mayonnaise with herbs

suprême	white sauce with chicken stock and cream
soubise	white onion sauce
verte	mayonnaise with spinach, watercress and herbs
vinaigrette	vinegar, gherkins and herbs

Game

coq au vin	chicken in red wine
canard à l'orange	duck and orange
canard montmorency	duck and cherries
canard à la serviette	boiled duck
civet de lièvre	hare stewed in red wine
caille	quail
côtelettes de chevreuil	venison cutlets
dindonneau farci	stuffed turkey
faisan à la choucroute	pheasant and pickled cabbage
faisan au riz basquaise	pheasant and Basque rice
lapin	rabbit
foie de volaille	chicken liver
oie rôtie	roast goose
pigeons en estouffade	stewed pigeons
poule au pot à la normande	poached chicken with cream
poule rôtie	roast chicken
poussins	young chickens
perdrix à l'auvergnate	partridge in white wine

râble de lièvre	saddle of hare
sarcelles rôties	roast teal

Vegetables

In France the vegetables are often served separately from the main dish because they are regarded as a dish on their own and are prepared accordingly. Fresh vegetables are essential to French taste and therefore many of the dishes are seasonal.

asperges à la mayonnaise	asparagus and mayonnaise
aubergines au gratin	aubergines baked with tomatoes and cheese
beignets d'aubergines	aubergine fritters
betteraves en robe de champs	baked beetroot
blettes à la crème	chard with cream sauce
carottes à la crème	carrots in cream sauce
céleris étuvés	celery stewed in butter
cèpes à la bordelaise	a kind of mushroom in oil and garlic
champignons à la crème	button mushrooms in cream
chanterelles maître d'hôtel	another kind of mushroom with butter and parsley
chou farci	stuffed cabbage
courgettes fines herbes	courgettes with herbs
endives au beurre	endives cooked in butter
épinards en purée	spinach purée
haricots à la bretonne	dried haricot beans cooked in wine

Eating and Drinking

haricots verts à la provençale	runner beans with tomatoes and garlic
lentilles au petit salé	lentils with salt pork
navets glacés	glazed turnips
oignons à l'étuvée	onions in wine
purée d'oseille	sorrel purée
petits pois au beurre	peas with butter
poireaux à la niçoise	leeks with oil and tomatoes
piments farcis	stuffed peppers
pommes lyonnaises	sauté potatoes and onions
pommes dauphinoises	fried potato balls
tomates provençales	tomatoes with breadcrumbs, garlic and parsley
topinambours à la crème	Jerusalem artichokes and cream

Desserts

The French are artists in confectionery and **gâteaux** but usually a selection of these are found only in the better restaurants. French people buy their **gâteaux** and **tartes** at the **pâtisseries** daily. At most places you will find the standard French desserts, which are listed here.

compote de fruits	stewed fruits
ananas au kirsch	pineapple and kirsch
poires étuvées	pears stewed in red wine
mousse au chocolat	chocolate mousse
glace au citron	lemon ice cream
omelette soufflée	a sweet omelette with liqueur

tarte aux fruits à l'alsacienne	Alsace fruit tart
tarte aux pommes	Normandy apple tart
crêpes	pancakes
gelée de groseilles	red currant jelly
bavarois	egg and cream custard flavoured with vanilla, coffee or chocolate
crème caramel	baked custard
St Honoré	flaky pastry, profiteroles and cream cake

Drinks

Aperitifs and wine are a part of the way of life of French-speaking Europe but the drinks most commonly used are cognac or one of the local **eaux de vie**, such as Marc of the Burgundy area. Most aperitifs are based on wine and have a slightly bitter-sweet taste, which is due to the herbs used in their manufacture. Amer Picon, Byrrh, Dubonnet and St Raphael are some of these. In Mediterranean areas aniseed-based aperitifs are the rule, such as Pernod and Ricard – both names well known throughout France. A pleasant aperitif which originates in Burgundy is Cassis – a dry white wine with blackcurrant liqueur.

A Dubonnet, please. with ice and lemon.	**Un Dubonnet s'il vous plaît. avec des glaçons et du citron.**
A whisky, please. on the rocks. with soda water. with water.	**Un whisky s'il vous plaît. avec glaçons. un whisky soda. à l'eau.**

Have you any non-alcoholic drinks?	**Avez-vous des boissons non-alcoolisées?**

Wine

Wine is an important matter to the French and there is a vast selection of wines of various categories. Most of these are subject to government control in order to maintain their quality. The best wines are vintage ones and are produced by well-known vineyards. In Bordeaux these are classified by the growths or **crus**. Classified wines include such prestigious names as Château Latour, Château Yquem and Château Lafite Rothschild. The types of wine are also classified by area, and **Appellation Contrôlée** means that the wine is guaranteed to be made from grapes in the area after which the wine is named. For example Médoc, Margaux and St Julien are among the Bordeaux wine-growing areas and Beaune, Côte d'Or, Côte de Nuits and Beaujolais are Burgundian areas. There are many other good wines in French-speaking Europe: Alsace, Loire and the wines of the Geneva region in Switzerland, such as Dôle, for example.

Often local wines are very good but they do not travel well and are therefore not exported.

The following list gives some of the better known wines, the growing regions and the wines they produce.

ALSACE

The wines from this area are named after the grape from which they are made and are mostly white and dry. Sylvaner, Riesling, Traminer, Gewurztraminer, Pinot, Tokay and Muscat are the best known.

BORDEAUX

Claret is one of the most popular types of French wine and
the great vintages have been classified since 1855. The main
wine-growing areas which give their names to types of wine
are Médoc, Graves, Sauterne, Entre deux Mers, St
Emilion, Pomerol, Fronsac and Blayas.

BURGUNDY

The main wine-growing areas are Chablis, Côte d'Or, Côte
de Nuits, Côte de Beaune, Côte Chalonnaise, Maconnais and
Beaujolais. The wines are red and white and mostly dry.

LANGUEDOC ROUSSILLON

This area of southern France produces the greatest volume
of wine. They are mostly table wines and predominantly
red and dry. There are also rosé wines.

PROVENCE

Wines of this region are dry and mostly drunk locally.

LOIRE

Muscadet at the mouth of the Loire river and Pouilly near
the source are the two famous wines of this region, which
produces many excellent white wines.

CHAMPAGNE

In some ways the most famous of all French wines, it is
produced in the vineyards around Rheims.

Soft Drinks

May we have some tea, please?
    a pot of tea.
    a lemon tea.
    China/Indian tea.

Du thé, s'il vous plaît.
    dans une théière.
    du thé au citron.
    du thé de Chine/de l'Inde.

A coffee with milk, please.

    with cream.
    a black coffee.
    iced coffee.

Un café au lait, s'il vous plaît.

    un café crème.
    un café noir.
    du café glacé.

I'd like an orange juice with soda water.
    a glass of cold milk.
    a long cool drink with plenty of ice.

    a milkshake.

Je voudrais un jus d'orange avec de l'eau minérale.
    un verre de lait froid.
    un grand verre d'une boisson bien fraîche avec des glaçons.
    un lait frappé.

Have you any lemonade?
    a bottle with a screw top?
    a straw?

Avez-vous de la limonade?
    une bouteille à vis?
    une paille?

VOCABULARY

beef tea	**du bouillon**
canned beer	**de la bière en boîte**
chocolate	**du chocolat**
cordial	**une liqueur**
cup	**une coupe**
lager	**une bière blonde**
syphon	**un syphon**
tonic	**un vin tonique**
tumbler	**un gobelet**

Shopping

Buying Food

Eating out is fun but so is buying food in the various types of food shops and markets. The French set great store by freshness and quality and the purchase of food is an important operation involving much discussion about the product.

At the Butcher's

What kind of meat is that?	**C'est quelle sorte de viande?**
What do you call that cut?	**Comment s'appelle ce morceau?**
I'd like some steaks please.	**Je voudrais des biftecks.**
How much does that weigh?	**Ça pèse combien?**
Will you please trim off the fat?	**Pourriez-vous ôter le gras?**
Will you take the meat off the bone?	**Pourriez-vous la désosser?**
Will you mince it?	**Pourriez-vous la hâcher?**
Please slice it very fine/thick.	**Pourriez-vous la couper en tranches très fines/épaisses?**
I'll have a little more.	**J'en veux un peu plus.**
That's too much.	**C'est trop.**
Put it in a plastic bag.	**Mettez-la dans un sachet en plastique.**
Cut it in cubes.	**Coupez-la en cubes.**

Vocabulary

beef	le boeuf
pot roast	un rôti à l'étouffée
rib of beef	la côte de boeuf
rump steak	le romsteck
roast beef	le rosbif
sirloin	le faux-filet
fillet of beef	le filet de boeuf
brains	la cervelle
cutlets	les côtelettes
cooking fat	de la graisse
escalopes	des escalopes
bacon	du lard
shoulder of lamb	l'épaule d'agneau
leg of lamb	le gigot d'agneau
liver	le foie
kidneys	les rognons
tongue	la langue
pigs' trotters	les pieds de cochon
leg of pork	le jambon frais
pork chop	la côtelette de porc
sweetbreads, veal/lamb	le ris de veau/d'agneau
sausages	les saucisses

At the Fishmonger's

Will you clean the fish?	Voulez-vous nettoyer le poisson?
Leave/take off the head/tail/fins, please.	Laissez/ôtez la tête/la queue/les nageoires, s'il vous plaît.
What is the name of that fish?	Comment s'appelle ce poisson?

The names of fish vary according to region, many fish having local names.

VOCABULARY

anchovies	**les anchois**
bass	**le bar**
bream	**la brème**
carp	**la carpe**
cod	**la morue/le cabillaud**
crayfish	**les écrevisses**
crab	**le crabe**
clam	**la palourde**
eel	**l'anguille**
herring	**le hareng**
lobster	**le homard**
mullet	**le mullet/le rouget**
mussels	**les moules**
oysters	**les huîtres**
octopus	**la poulpe**
perch	**la perche**
pike	**le brochet**
plaice	**la plie/le carrelet**
prawns	**les crevettes**
salmon	**le saumon**
sardines	**les sardines**
sole	**la sole**
squid	**le calmar**
trout	**la truite**
tunny	**le thon**
turbot	**le turbot**
whitebait	**la blanchaille**

At the Delicatessen/Dairy

What kinds of sausage have you got?	**Quelles sortes de saucisses avez-vous?**

I'd like a peppery one.	J'en voudrais au poivre.
one without garlic.	sans aïl.
one not too highly seasoned.	qui ne soit pas trop assaisonnée.
I prefer a coarse/smooth pâté.	Je préfère un pâté haché gros/fin.
game pâté.	un pâté de gibier.
What is the name of that cheese?	Comment s'appelle ce fromage?
Have you any goat's cheese?	Avez-vous du fromage de chèvre?
Do I have to take the whole cheese or will you cut me a piece?	Faut-il acheter tout le fromage ou pouvez-vous m'en couper un morceau?
May I taste it for ripeness?	Est-ce que je peux goûter pour voir s'il est bien fait?
Have you any biscuits/sweet biscuits/water biscuits?	Avez-vous des biscuits/des biscuits sucrés/non sucrés?
Do you sell breakfast cereals?	Avez-vous des céréales/corn-flakes?
I'll take a little of each salad.	Je prendrai un peu de chaque salade.
Have you a tube of tomato purée?	Avez-vous de la purée de tomate en tube?
Have you a jar of olives?	Avez-vous un bocal d'olives?

Vocabulary

chitterling	**les andouilles**
dried beef	**la viande séchée**
faggots	**les boulettes de viande**
garlic sausage	**du saucisson à l'ail**
ham	**du jambon**
macaroni	**les macaronis**
olives	**les olives**
gherkins	**les cornichons**
quiche	**la quiche**
spaghetti	**les spaghettis**
smoked fish	**le poisson fumé**
tinned food	**les conserves**

Cheeses

Bleu de Bresse	a strong, sharp cheese
Brie	a soft, creamy cheese
Camembert	a rich, strong creamy cheese
Cantal	a well-flavoured cheese
Emmenthal	a mild, firm cheese
Gruyère	a good flavoured, firm cheese
Pont l'Evêque	a tasty, smooth cheese

At the Grocer's/Supermarket

bacon	**le lard/le bacon**
bread	**le pain**
brush	**la brosse/le pinceau**
bottle (of)	**la bouteille (de)**
butter	**le beurre**
biscuits	**les biscuits**
cereals	**les cornflakes/les céréales**
cleaning fluid	**le produit à nettoyer**
crisps	**les chips**
detergent	**le détergent**

Buying Food

dried fruit	**les fruits secs**
disinfectant	**le désinfectant**
duster	**le torchon à épousseter**
eggs	**les oeufs**
flour	**la farine**
jam	**la confiture**
jar (of)	**le bocal (de)**
margarine	**la margarine**
oil	**l'huile**
paper napkins	**les serviettes de papier**
pepper	**le poivre**
rice	**le riz**
salt	**le sel**
tin (of)	**la boîte (de)**
vinegar	**le vinaigre**
washing powder	**la lessive**

At the Greengrocer and Fruiterer's

Is the melon ripe?	**Le melon est mûr?**
How many will make a kilo?	**Combien y en a t-il dans un kilo?**
It's for eating today/tomorrow.	**C'est pour manger aujourd'hui/demain.**
Will you please weigh this?	**Pouvez-vous peser ça?**
This lettuce is not very fresh.	**Cette laitue n'est pas très fraîche.**
Are these apples crisp?	**Ces pommes sont croquantes?**
Have you got a stronger bag?	**Avez-vous un sac plus solide?**
I will put it in my carrier.	**Je vais le mettre dans mon sac.**

Have you got a box?	**Avez-vous une boîte en carton?**

VOCABULARY

apples	**les pommes**
apricots	**les abricots**
artichoke	**l'artichaut**
asparagus	**les asperges**
banana	**la banane**
beans, broad	**les fèves**
French	**les haricots verts**
runner	**les haricots d'Espagne**
beetroot	**la betterave rouge**
blackberry	**la mûre**
broccoli	**le brocoli**
cabbage	**le choux**
carrots	**les carottes**
cauliflower	**le choux-fleur**
cherry	**la cerise**
chestnut	**la châtaigne/le marron**
cress	**le cresson**
cucumber	**le concombre**
date	**la datte**
fig	**la figue**
grapefruit	**le pamplemousse**
grapes	**les raisins**
greengages	**les reines-claude**
hazelnuts	**les noisettes**
leeks	**les poireaux**
lemons	**les citrons**
lettuce	**la laitue**
melon	**le melon**
onions	**les oignons**
oranges	**les oranges**

peaches	**les pêches**
pears	**les poires**
peas	**les petits pois**
pineapple	**l'ananas**
plums	**les prunes**
potatoes	**les pommes de terre**
radishes	**les radis**
raspberry	**les framboises**
rhubarb	**la rhubarbe**
spinach	**les épinards**
strawberries	**les fraises**
sweet corn	**le maïs**
sweet pepper	**les poivrons**
tangerines	**les mandarines**
tomatoes	**les tomates**
turnips	**les navets**

Other Shops

Napoleon said that the British were a nation of shopkeepers, but nowhere are there more individually owned shops than in France. This makes shopping a pleasure for its variety as well as for the unique character of each establishment. Most shops are open from 9.00 to 18.00 hours and even later in summer, but shut for lunch between 12.00 and 14.00 or even 15.00. Sunday is often a working day, but on Monday many shops close.

I want to go shopping. Where are the best shops?	**Je veux faire des achats. Où sont les meilleurs magasins?**
the most popular shops?	**les magasins les plus populaires?**
the cheaper shops?	**les magasins les moins chers?**
Where is the market?	**Où est le marché?**

Until what time are you open?	**Vous restez ouverts jusqu'à quelle heure?**
Is there a grocer's near here?	**Y a-t-il une épicerie près d'ici?**

VOCABULARY

antique shop	**l'antiquaire**
art gallery	**la galerie d'art**
baker	**la boulangerie**
bank	**la banque**
beauty salon	**le salon de coiffure**
bookshop	**la librairie**
butcher	**la boucherie**
chemist	**la pharmacie**
confectionery	**la confiserie**
dairy	**la crèmerie**
delicatessen	**la charcuterie**
department store	**le grand magasin**
dry cleaner	**le pressing/le nettoyage à sec**
fishmonger	**la poissonnerie**
greengrocer	**le marchand de légumes**
grocer	**l'épicerie**
hairdresser	**le coiffeur**
hardware store	**la quincaillerie**
jeweller	**le bijoutier**
newsagent	**le marchand de journaux**
off licence	**le débit de boissons**
optician	**l'opticien**
photographer	**le photographe**
shoemaker	**le cordonnier**
shoe shop	**le marchand de chaussures**
stationer	**la papeterie**
tailor	**le tailleur**
tobacconist	**le débit de tabac**
toy shop	**le magasin de jouets**

Shopping

travel agency	**l'agence de voyages**
watchmaker	**l'horlogerie**
wine merchant	**le marchand de vin**

Buying Clothes

I'm just looking, thank you.	**Je ne fais que regarder. Merci.**
I would like to see some shirts.	**Je voudrais voir des chemises.**
plain/coloured/striped.	**unies/de couleur/ rayées.**
with long/short sleeves.	**à manches longues/ courtes.**
in cotton.	**en coton.**
My size is ...	**Je porte du ...**
My collar size is ...	**Mon tour de cou est ...**
This colour does not suit me.	**Cette couleur ne me va pas.**
It is not my style.	**Ce n'est pas mon genre.**
I want something more casual.	**Je veux quelque chose de moins habillé.**
Can I return it if it is unsuitable?	**Est-ce que je peux le rapporter si ça ne convient pas?**
May I have a receipt?	**Pouvez-vous me donner un reçu?**
It does not fit.	**Ça ne me va pas.**
It is too large/small/narrow/ wide.	**C'est trop grand/petit/étroit/ large.**
Can you show me something else?	**Pouvez-vous me montrer autre chose?**

MATERIALS

camel hair	poil de chameau
chiffon	mousseline de soie
cotton	coton
crepe	crêpe de chine
denim	serge de coton
felt	feutre
flannel	flannelle
gaberdine	gabardine
lace	dentelle
leather	cuir
linen	lin
materials	tissus
nylon	nylon
piqué	piqué
poplin	popeline
rayon	rayonne
satin	satin
silk	soie
suede	daim
tweed	tweed
taffeta	taffetas
velvet	velours
velour	velours de laine
wool	laine
worsted	laine peignée

MEASUREMENTS

arm	longueur de manche
leg	longueur de jambe
chest	tour de poitrine
waist	tour de taille
neck	tour de cou
hip	tour de hanche

COLOURS

black	**noir(e)**
blue	**bleu(e)**
biscuit	**biscuit**
green	**vert(e)**
mauve	**mauve**
pastel colours	**couleurs pastel**
orange	**orange**
red	**rouge**
rose	**rose**
strong colours	**couleurs vives**
violet	**violet**
white	**blanc(che)**
yellow	**jaune**

ITEMS OF CLOTHING

anorak	**un anorak**
bathing hat	**un bonnet de bain**
bathrobe	**un peignoir**
belt	**une ceinture**
blazer	**un blazer**
blouse	**une blouse/un chemisier**
boots	**des bottes/de grosses chaussures**
bra	**un soutien-gorge**
briefs	**un slip**
buckle	**une boucle**
button	**un bouton**
cap	**une casquette**
cardigan	**un cardigan**
coat	**un manteau**
dinner jacket	**un smoking**
dress	**une robe**
elastic	**de l'élastique**
girdle	**une gaine**
gloves	**des gants**
gym shoes	**des chaussures de gymnastique**

handkerchief	un mouchoir
hat	un chapeau
hook and eye	une agrafe
jacket	une veste
jeans	un jean
jumper	un chandail
negligé	un négligé
nightdress	une chemise de nuit
overcoat	un pardessus
panties	une culotte
pants suit	un ensemble-pantalon
pocket	une poche
press stud	un bouton-pression
pullover	un pull
pyjamas	un pyjama
raincoat	un imperméable
sandals	des sandales
scarf	un foulard
shirt	une chemise
shoelaces	des lacets
shoes	des chaussures
shorts	un short
skirt	une jupe
slip	une combinaison
slippers	des pantoufles
stockings	des bas
suit (man's)	un complet
suit (woman's)	un tailleur
suspenders	des bretelles
swimsuit	un maillot de bain
T-shirt	une T-shirt
thread	du fil
tie	une cravate
tights	un collant
trousers	un pantalon
twinset	un twinset
underpants	un slip

vest	**un maillot de corps**
waistcoat	**un gilet**
zip	**une fermeture éclair**

At the Shoe Shop

I want a pair of walking shoes.	**Je veux une paire de chaussures de marche.**
evening shoes.	**de souliers du soir.**
moccasins.	**de mocassins.**
boots.	**de bottes (de grosses chaussures).**
suede shoes.	**de chaussures de daim.**
slippers.	**de pantoufles.**
sandals.	**de sandales.**
canvas shoes.	**de chaussures de toile.**
My size is ...	**Ma pointure est ...**
I need a broad/narrow fitting.	**Il me faut une chaussure large/étroite.**
I want high/low heels.	**Je veux des talons hauts/bas.**
flat-heeled shoes.	**des chaussures à talon plat.**
leather-soled/rubber-soled/cork-soled shoes.	**des chaussures à semelle de cuir/de caoutchouc/de liège.**
These are not comfortable.	**Celles-ci ne sont pas confortables.**
May I try the other shoe?	**Je peux essayer l'autre chaussure?**
Have you got a shoehorn?	**Avez-vous un chausse-pied?**
They are not my style.	**Ce n'est pas mon genre.**

Have you any other colours?	**Avez-vous d'autres couleurs?**
How much are they?	**Elles coûtent combien?**
That is more than I want to pay.	**C'est plus que je ne veux dépenser.**
I will keep them on. Will you please wrap up my own shoes?	**Je les garde aux pieds. Voulez-vous emballer mes chaussures?**
Do you sell shoe polish/shoe cleaner/shoe brushes?	**Avez-vous du cirage/du produit de nettoyage/des brosses à chaussures?**

Tobacconist's

Have you any English cigarettes?	**Avez-vous des cigarettes anglaises?**
What brand is the most popular here?	**Qu'est-ce qu'on fume le plus ici?**
Are they Virginian or French/Egyptian/Turkish/American tobacco?	**Est-ce qu'elles contiennent du tabac de Virginie ou du tabac français/egyptien/turc/américain?**
Have you any filter tips/king size/menthol cooled?	**Avez-vous des cigarettes à bout filtre/longues/mentholées?**
Do you sell pipe tobacco?	**Avez-vous du tabac pour la pipe?**
May I see your selection of pipes?	**Montrez-moi ce que vous avez comme pipes.**
I'd like a cigar.	**Je voudrais un cigare.**

Shopping

Do you sell pipe cleaners?	**Avez-vous des cure-pipes?**
A packet/carton of . . . cigarettes, please.	**Un paquet/une cartouche de cigarettes . . . s'il vous plaît.**
A box of matches, please.	**Une boîte d'allumettes s'il vous plaît.**

VOCABULARY

box	**une boîte**
case	**un étui**
cigarette lighter	**un briquet**
cleaners	**des cure-pipes**
carton	**une cartouche de cigarettes**
gas	**le gaz**
lighter fluid	**de l'essence à briquet**
flint	**un silex**
matches	**des allumettes**
pouch	**une blague**
pipe	**une pipe**
packet	**un paquet**

Hardware Store and Electrical Goods

I'd like a heavy-duty saucepan/frying pan.	**Je voudrais une casserole solide/une poêle à frire.**
Have you a grill/charcoal?	**Avez-vous un gril/du charbon de bois?**
I need a metal/plastic can for water.	**Je voudrais un bidon en métal/en plastique pour l'eau.**
I should like a bucket.	**Je voudrais un seau.**

Give me a ball of strong twine.	**Donnez-moi une pelote de ficelle.**
I need a tow rope and a hook.	**Il me faut une corde pour remorquer la voiture et un crochet.**
I need a battery for my torch/radio.	**Il me faut une pile pour ma lampe de poche/ma radiò.**

VOCABULARY

adaptor	**un raccord**
basket	**un panier**
battery	**une batterie**
brush	**une brosse/un pinceau**
bulb	**une ampoule**
car radio	**une radio pour la voiture**
chamois leather	**une peau de chamois**
distilled water	**de l'eau distillée**
duster	**un torchon**
fork	**une fourchette**
hammer	**un marteau**
insulating tape	**du chatterton**
knife	**un couteau**
mallet	**un maillet**
penknife	**un canif**
percolator	**un percolateur**
saw	**une scie**
scissors	**des ciseaux**
screwdriver	**un tournevis**
spoon	**une cuillère**
string	**de la ficelle**
tweezers	**des petites pinces**
wire	**du fil de fer**
wrench	**une clé à écrous/clé à molette**

Chemist's

Do I need a doctor's prescription?	Est-ce qu'il me faut une ordonnance?
Is there an all-night chemist open?	Y a-t-il une pharmacie qui fait service de nuit?
Can you make up this prescription?	Pouvez-vous me préparer cette ordonnance?
When will it be ready?	Quand est-ce que ce sera prêt?
Will you write down the instructions in English if possible?	Pouvez-vous m'inscrire le mode d'emploi, en anglais si possible?
Is this all right/dangerous for children?	C'est approprié/dangereux pour les enfants?
Have you anything for a cold?	Avez-vous quelque chose pour soigner un rhume?
sore throat?	un mal de gorge?
a cough?	une toux?
I'd like to buy a thermometer.	Je voudrais un thermomètre.
Would you please have a look at this cut/bruise?	Pourriez-vous examiner cette coupure/contusion?
What kind of bandage would be best?	Quel pansement conviendrait le mieux?
I've got an upset stomach.	J'ai l'estomac dérangé.
diarrhoea.	de la diarrhée.
indigestion.	une indigestion.
a headache.	des maux de tête.
sunburn.	un coup de soleil.
I am constipated.	Je suis constipé.

Vocabulary

Medicines

aspirin	l'aspirine
antibiotic	l'antibiotique
bandage	le pansement
band-aids	le sparadrap
contraceptive	le contraceptif
corn plaster	des emplâtres pour les cors
cough mixture	un expectorant
cough lozenges	des pastilles pour la toux
cotton wool	du coton hydrophile
disinfectant	le désinfectant
ear drops	les gouttes pour les oreilles
gargle	le gargarisme
gauze	la gaze
insect repellant	l'insectifuge
iodine	l'iode
iron pills	les pastilles au fer
laxative	le laxatif
lip salve	la pommade pour les lèvres
sanitary towels	les serviettes hygiéniques
sedative	le sédatif
sleeping pills	le somnifère
tranquillizers	le calmant
thermometer	le thermomètre
vitamins	les vitamines

Toilet articles

after-shave	de la lotion après-rasage
bath salts	des sels de bain
bath oil	de l'huile pour le bain
cologne	de l'eau de cologne
cream, cleansing	une crème démaquillante
cuticle	traitante pour les ongles
foundation	du fond de teint

Shopping

moisturising	**hydratante**
deodorant	**un désodorisant**
emery board	**une lime à ongles**
eye pencil	**un crayon pour les yeux**
eye shadow	**du fard à paupière**
face pack	**un masque anti-rides**
face powder	**de la poudre**
lipstick	**du rouge à lèvres**
nailbrush	**une brosse à ongles**
nail file	**une lime à ongles**
nail polish	**du vernis à ongles**
nail polish remover	**du dissolvant**
perfume	**du parfum**
razor	**un rasoir**
rouge	**du fard à joues**
safety pins	**des épingles de sûreté**
shampoo	**du shampooing**
shaving cream	**de la crème à raser**
shaving brush	**un blaireau**
soap	**du savon**
suntan oil	**de l'huile solaire**
sponge	**une éponge**
tissues	**des mouchoirs en papier**
toilet paper	**du papier hygiénique**
toothpaste	**du dentifrice**
toothbrush	**une brosse à dents**

At the Photographer's

I'd like to buy a camera.	**Je voudrais acheter un appareil de photos.**
One that is cheap and easy to use.	**Un appareil bon marché et facile à utiliser.**
Will you please check my camera?	**Pouvez-vous vérifier mon appareil?**

The film is stuck.	**Le film est coincé.**
The exposure meter is not working.	**Le posemètre ne marche pas.**
The flash does not light up.	**L'ampoule flash ne s'allume pas.**
The film winder is jammed.	**Le levier d'avancement est bloqué.**
Can you do it soon?	**Pouvez-vous le faire bientôt?**
Will you please process this film?	**Pouvez-vous développer ce film?**
I want some black and white/ colour film.	**Je veux une pellicule noir et blanc/en couleurs.**
Is this film for use in daylight or artificial light?	**Est-ce que cette pellicule convient pour la lumière du jour ou la lumière artificielle?**
I need a light meter.	**Il me faut une cellule photo-électrique.**
How much is an electronic flash?	**Combien coûte un flash électronique?**

VOCABULARY

films 120/127/135/620	**six-six (6 × 6)/quatre-quatre (4 × 4)/vingt-quatre trente-six (24 × 36)/six-cent vingt**
20 exposures/36 exposures/ a fast film/a fine grain film/ cine film 8mm/16mm	**vingt poses/trente-six poses/ ultra rapide/à grain fin/film pour caméra huit millimètres/seize millimètres**

Shopping

flash bulb	**une ampoule flash**
lens	**la lentille**
lens cap	**le capuchon pour objectif**
red filter	**le filtre rouge**
yellow filter	**le filtre jaune**
ultra violet	**ultra violet**
range finder	**le télémètre**
shutter	**l'obturateur**
reflex camera	**l'appareil photo-réflexe**
long-focus lens	**le télé-objectif**
wide-angle lens	**l'objectif grand angle**
camera case	**l'étui**

Bookshop/Stationer's

On which shelf are the books on art/history/politics/sport?	**Où se trouvent les livres sur l'art/l'histoire/la politique/le sport?**
Where are the guide books?	**Où se trouvent les guides?**
I want a pocket dictionary.	**Je voudrais un dictionnaire de poche.**
Have you any English paperbacks?	**Avez-vous des livres de poche en anglais?**
Can you recommend an easy-to-read book in French?	**Pouvez-vous recommander un livre en français, facile à lire?**
One with plenty of illustrations.	**Un livre bien illustré.**
Do you sell second-hand books?	**Avez-vous des livres d'occasion?**
I want a map of the area.	**Je voudrais une carte de la région.**
The scale of this one is too small.	**Cette carte est à une trop petite échelle.**

Have you got refills for this ballpoint pen?	**Avez-vous une recharge pour ce stylo à bille?**
Can you please keep the English newspaper for me every morning?	**Pouvez-vous me garder le journal anglais chaque matin?**

VOCABULARY

address book	**un carnet d'adresses**
box of crayons	**une boîte de crayons de couleur**
carbon paper	**du papier carbone**
cellophane	**de la cellophane**
drawing paper	**du papier à dessiner**
envelopes	**des enveloppes**
exercise book	**un cahier**
fountain pen	**un stylo à encre**
greaseproof paper	**du papier sulfurisé**
glue	**de la colle**
ink	**de l'encre**
label	**une étiquette**
notebook	**un carnet**
notepaper	**du papier à lettres**
paste	**de la colle blanche**
pen	**une plume**
pencil	**un crayon**
pencil sharpener	**un taille-crayon**
playing cards	**des cartes à jouer**
rubber	**une gomme**
ruler	**une règle**
silver foil	**du papier d'aluminium**
typewriter ribbon	**un ruban pour machine à écrire**
typing paper	**du papier pour machine à écrire**
writing pad	**un bloc-note**

Buying Souvenirs

Are all these things made in France?	**Est-ce que tous ces objets sont fabriqués en France?**
This is a nice straw hat.	**Voilà un beau chapeau de paille.**
I like this bag.	**Ce sac me plaît.**
Have you any costume jewellery?	**Avez-vous des bijoux en métal non-précieux?**
I'm looking for bracelet charms.	**Je cherche des breloques pour un bracelet.**
I'd like to try on that ring.	**Je voudrais essayer cette bague.**
What is this bracelet made of?	**En quoi est ce bracelet?**
I collect copperware. Have you any pots?	**Je collectionne des objets en cuivre. Avez-vous des pots de cuivre?**
I'd like some local pottery.	**Je voudrais de la poterie locale.**
Can you pack this carefully?	**Pouvez-vous bien m'emballer ça?**
Do you despatch things abroad?	**Expédiez-vous des marchandises à l'étranger?**
I'm just looking around.	**Je jette simplement un coup d'oeil.**
I will come back later.	**Je reviendrai plus tard.**
Can I leave a deposit on it and return tomorrow?	**Est-ce que je peux vous payer un acompte et revenir demain?**

| Do you take foreign cheques with a Eurocard? | Acceptez-vous des chèques étrangers avec une Eurocarte? |

VOCABULARY

beads	des perles
brooch	une broche
chain	une chaîne
cigarette lighter	un briquet
clock	une pendule/une horloge
cuff links	des boutons de manchette
earrings	des boucles d'oreille
jewel box	une boîte à bijoux
music box	une boîte à musique
necklace	un collier
rosary	un chapelet
silverware	l'argenterie
watchstrap	un bracelet de montre
wristwatch	une montre-bracelet

Entertainment

Out for the Evening

Nightclubs

Can you recommend a nightclub with a good show?	Pouvez-vous recommander une boîte de nuit avec un bon 'show'?
a place with dancing and a cabaret?	un endroit avec dancing et cabaret?
a disco?	une discothèque?
an open-air dance?	une dancing en plein air?
a nightclub with hostesses?	une boîte de nuit avec hôtesses?
Is there an entrance fee?	Faut-il payer pour entrer?
Does it include drinks?	Est-ce que les boissons sont comprises?
What is the cost of drinks?	Combien coûtent les boissons?
At what time does the show start?	A quelle heure commence le 'show'?
Is there a different price for drinks at the bar?	Est-ce que les prix sont différents au bar?
I do not want a photograph.	Je ne veux pas de photo.
May I have this dance?	Voulez-vous m'accorder cette danse?

Cinemas

What is on at the cinema?	Quels films passent au cinéma en ce moment?

Have you got a guide to what's on?	**Avez-vous un guide des programmes?**
Two stalls/circle/amphitheatre, please.	**Deux fauteuils d'orchestre/ de balcon/d'amphithéatre, s'il vous plaît.**
Will we have to queue for long?	**Faut-il faire la queue pendant longtemps?**
I want a seat near the front/at the back/in the middle.	**Je veux une place à l'avant/à l'arrière/au milieu.**
Do I tip the usherette?	**Je donne un pourboire à l'ouvreuse?**
I'd rather sit over there.	**Je préfèrerais m'asseoir là-bas.**
Will you please shine your torch here?	**Pouvez-vous éclairer ici?**
I have dropped something.	**J'ai fait tomber quelque chose.**
Do they sell ice-cream?	**On vend des glaces?**
At what time does the main film start?	**A quelle heure commence le film principal?**
Will you please move over to the right/left.	**Poussez-vous un peu à droite/ à gauche, s'il vous plaît.**

VOCABULARY

actor	**l'acteur**
actress	**l'actrice**
director	**le metteur en scène**
dubbing	**le doublage**

Entertainment

interval	l'entracte
producer	le réalisateur
projector	le projecteur
screen	l'écran
sound	le son
star	la vedette

Concert Hall

I want a seat from which I can see the pianist's hands.	Je veux une place d'où je peux voir les mains du pianiste.
Can I buy the score?	Est-ce qu'on peut acheter la partition?
Who is conducting tonight?	Qui est le chef d'orchestre ce soir?
Who is the soloist?	Qui est le soliste?

VOCABULARY

bass	la basse
bassoon	le basson
brass	les cuivres
cello	le violoncelle
clarinet	la clarinette
cymbal	la cymbale
drum	le tambour
French horn	le cor d'harmonie
flute	la flûte
percussion	les instruments à percussion
saxophone	le saxophone
strings	les instruments à corde
trombone	le trombone

timpani	**les timbales**
trumpet	**la trompette**
violin	**le violon**
wind	**les instruments à vent**

Theatre/Opera

Is there a ticket agency near?	**Y a-t-il une agence tout près?**
Can one get tickets anywhere else?	**Peut-on acheter les billets ailleurs?**
Are there any last-minute returns?	**Y a-t-il des retours à la dernière minute?**
Do we have to wear evening dress?	**La tenue de soirée est-elle de rigueur?**
I'd like a souvenir programme.	**Je voudrais un programme comme souvenir.**
What is the name of the prima donna?	**Quel est le nom de la prima donna?**
Who is the leading actor?	**Qui joue le rôle principal?**
How long is the interval?	**Combien de temps dure l'entracte?**
Where is the bar?	**Où est le bar?**

Vocabulary

applause	**l'applaudissement**
audience	**le public**
bass	**la basse**
baritone	**le baryton**

Entertainment

composer	**le compositeur**
conductor	**le chef d'orchestre**
contralto	**le contralto**
encore	**bis**
orchestra	**l'orchestre**
playwright	**l'auteur**
scenery	**le décor**
soprano	**la soprano**
stage	**la scène**
tenor	**le tenor**

Casino

What games are played here?	**Quelles sortes de jeux sont proposés ici?**
What is the minimum stake in this room?	**Quelle est la mise minimum dans cette salle?**
Can I buy some chips?	**Puis-je acheter des jetons?**
I should like 100 francs' worth.	**J'en voudrais pour cent francs.**
Excuse me, those are my chips.	**Excusez-moi, ce sont mes jetons.**
Where can I cash my chips?	**Où est-ce que je peux toucher mes jetons?**
I'm bust/that's the end of the game for me!	**Le jeu s'arrête là pour moi.**
I'll take another card.	**Une autre carte.**
No more.	**Ça suffit.**
Pass me the dice, please.	**Passez-moi les dés, s'il vous plaît.**

Vocabulary

ace	l'as
bet	le pari
blackjack	le pouilleux
cards	les cartes
chemin de fer	chemin de fer
clubs	trèfle
croupier	le croupier
diamonds	carreau
evens	pair
hearts	coeur
jack	le valet
joker	joker
king	le roi
poker	poker
queen	la reine
shoe	la pelle
spades	pique

Out for the Day

On the Beach

Does one have to pay to use this beach? — Est-ce qu'il faut payer pour aller sur cette plage?

Is there a free section of the beach? — Est-ce qu'une partie de la plage est gratuite?

Is it clean? — C'est propre?

How much does it cost per day/per week to hire a cabin? — Combien coûte par jour/par semaine la location d'une cabine?

  deckchair? —   d'un transat?

air mattress?	**d'un matelas pneumatique?**
sun umbrella?	**d'un parasol?**
Can I leave valuables in the cabin?	**Est-ce qu'on peut laisser les objets de valeur dans la cabine?**
Is the ticket valid all day?	**Est-ce que ce ticket est valable pour toute la journée?**
Does the beach slope steeply?	**Est-ce que la plage est très en pente?**
Is it safe for swimming?	**Est-ce qu'on peut nager sans danger?**
Are there any currents?	**Y a-t-il des courants?**
Is it safe to dive off the rocks?	**Peut-on plonger des rochers sans danger?**
Where is the fresh-water shower?	**Où est la douche d'eau fraîche?**
Have you any tar remover?	**Avez-vous un produit pour enlever le goudron?**
Can I hire a swimsuit/trunks?	**Est-ce qu'on peut louer un maillot de bain/un slip?**
I've hurt my foot. Have you any elastoplast?	**Je me suis fait mal au pied. Avez-vous du sparadrap?**
Is there a lost property office?	**Y a-t-il un bureau d'objets trouvés?**
Is there a children's beach club?	**Y a-t-il un club pour enfants sur la plage?**
At what time are the keep fit classes?	**A quelle heure ont lieu les cours de gymnastique?**

Is there water ski tuition available?	Y a-t-il des classes de ski nautique?
Does it matter if I can't swim?	Je ne sais pas nager. Est-ce que ça fait quelque chose?
Where is the nearest beach shop?	Où est la boutique d'articles pour la plage la plus proche?
Have you got a life jacket?	Avez-vous une ceinture de sauvetage?
Is this a good place for skin diving?	Est-ce que c'est un bon endroit pour faire de la plongée sous-marine?
Help! I'm in difficulty.	Au secours! Je suis en difficulté.

VOCABULARY

beach ball	un ballon
cactus	un cactus
goggles	des lunettes protectrices
harpoon gun	un fusil harpon
high tide	la marée haute
low tide	la marée basse
lilo	un matelas pneumatique
net	un filet
promenade	le quai
pedalo	un pédalo
pines	des pins
raft	un radeau
rocks	des rochers
rowing boat	un bateau à rames
sand	le sable
sandals	des sandales
sea	la mer

Sightseeing

seaweed	des algues
shells	des coquillages
shingle	des galets
sun oil	de l'huile solaire
surf	le ressac
surf board	une planche de surfing
underwater	sous-marin
waterski instructor	le moniteur de ski nautique
yacht	un yacht

Sightseeing

Where can I get a good guide book?	Où est-ce que je peux acheter un bon guide?
Is there an excursion round the city?	Y a-t-il un tour de la ville organisé?
Is it a conducted party?	Est-ce que c'est une visite organisée?
Am I allowed to go round alone?	Est-ce que je peux visiter sans guide?
Where do I find an official guide?	Où peut-on trouver un guide officiel?
Does the excursion price include lunch?	Est-ce que le déjeuner est inclus dans le prix de l'excursion?
Are the entrance fees extra?	Est-ce que le prix des entrées est en plus?
Should I tip the guide/driver?	Faut-il donner un pourboire au guide/au chauffeur?
I'd like to stay here longer.	J'aimerais bien rester ici plus longtemps.

I'll meet the party later.	**Je rejoindrai le groupe plus tard.**
Where will you be?	**Où serez-vous?**
Will you please write it down?	**Pouvez-vous me l'écrire?**
Can I hire an audioguide?	**Est-ce qu'on peut louer un audioguide?**

In Churches

Do ladies have to cover their heads?	**Est-ce que les dames doivent se couvrir les cheveux?**
Is it all right to enter like this?	**Je peux entrer comme ça?**
How old is this church?	**De quand date cette église?**
Who founded it?	**Par qui a-t-elle été fondée?**
Are the stained glass windows original?	**Les vitraux sont de l'époque?**
Can one illuminate the fresco?	**Peut-on illuminer la fresque?**
Is one allowed to go up the bell tower?	**Peut-on monter dans le clocher?**
Is there a book about the church?	**Existe-t-il un livre sur l'église?**
May I leave a small contribution?	**Est-ce que je peux donner un peu d'argent?**

VOCABULARY

abbey	**l'abbaye**
aisles	**le bas-côté**

115

Sightseeing

altar	l'autel
arch	l'arche
basilica	la basilique
candle	la bougie
cathedral	la cathédrale
chapel	la chapelle
cloister	le cloître
crucifix	le crucifix
crypt	la crypte
convent	le couvent
choir	le choeur
column	la colonne
fresco	la fresque
font	les fonts baptismaux
monastery	le monastère
nave	la nef
rood	le crucifix central
sculpture	la sculpture
shrine	la châsse
west front	la façade ouest

Art Galleries and Museums

Have you a catalogue/illustrated catalogue?	Avez-vous un catalogue/un catalogue illustré?
Are there any plaster casts?	Y a-t-il des moulages au plâtre?
Do you sell transparencies?	Avez-vous des diapositives?
Am I allowed to take photographs?	Est-ce qu'on peut prendre des photos?
May I use my tripod?	Est-ce que je peux me servir d'un trépied?

Is the gallery open on Sundays?	**Est-ce que la galerie est ouverte le dimanche?**
Is it free?	**L'entrée est gratuite?**
Where can I find the Dutch School?	**Où se trouve l'école hollandaise?**
Do you make photocopies?	**Faites-vous des photocopies?**
Where is the library?	**Où est la bibliothèque?**

VOCABULARY

antique books	**les livres anciens**
bas relief	**le bas-relief**
china	**la porcelaine**
costumes	**les costumes**
drawing	**les dessins**
engraving	**la gravure**
etching	**la gravure à l'eau-forte**
frame	**le cadre**
furniture	**les meubles**
jewellery	**les bijoux**
lithograph	**la lithographie**
miniature	**la miniature**
porcelain	**la porcelaine**
pottery	**la poterie/la céramique**
silverware	**l'argenterie**

Historical Sights

Will there be far to walk?	**Y a-t-il loin à marcher?**
Can I wait here till you return?	**Je peux vous attendre ici?**

Sightseeing

Is there a souvenir stall?	**Est-ce qu'on vend des souvenirs?**
Where can we get a cold drink?	**Où peut-on trouver des boissons fraîches?**
Is there a plan of the grounds?	**Y a-t-il un plan du parc?**
I would like to walk round the gardens.	**Je voudrais faire le tour des jardins.**

VOCABULARY

arena	**l'arène**
aquaduct	**l'aqueduc**
amphitheatre	**l'amphithéatre**
armour	**l'armure**
battlements	**les créneaux**
catacombs	**les catacombes**
cannon	**le canon**
castle	**le château**
courtyard	**la cour**
column	**la colonne**
crossbow	**l'arbalète**
fort	**le fort**
forum	**le forum**
fountain	**la fontaine**
fortifications	**les fortifications**
gate	**la porte**
portcullis	**la herse**
pediment	**le fronton**
viaduct	**le viaduc**
wall	**le mur**

Gardens

Are these gardens open to the public?	**Est-ce que ces jardins sont ouverts au public?**
Can we walk where we like?	**Est-ce qu'on peut aller où l'on veut?**
How long will it take to walk around?	**Combien de temps faut-il pour faire tout le tour?**
At what time do you close?	**A quelle heure fermez-vous?**
Is there a plan of the gardens?	**Y a-t-il un plan des jardins?**
Where are the greenhouses?	**Où sont les serres?**
Where is the tropical plant house?	**Où est la serre des plantes tropicales?**
May we sit on the grass?	**On peut s'asseoir sur l'herbe?**
What is the name of that plant/flower?	**Comment s'appelle cette plante/cette fleur?**
Is there a lake/pond?	**Y a-t-il un lac/un bassin?**
Who designed these gardens?	**Qui a dessiné ces jardins?**

VOCABULARY

ash	**le frêne**
beech	**le hêtre**
birch	**le bouleau**
bougainvillea	**la bougainvillée**
carnation	**l'oeillet**
chrysanthemum	**le chrysanthème**
cherry tree	**le cerisier**
clematis	**la clématite**

Sightseeing

daffodil	la jonquille
dahlia	le dahlia
daisy	la marguerite
deciduous trees	les arbres à feuilles caduques
elm	l'orme
evergreen	les arbres à feuilles persistantes
fir	le sapin
geranium	le géranium
herbaceous border	la bordure herbacée
ivy	le lierre
lily	le lys
moss	la mousse
nasturtium	la capucine
oak	le chêne
pear tree	le poirier
pine	le pin
plane	le platane
poplar	le peuplier
rose	la rose
tulip	la tulipe
violet	la violette
wisteria	la glycine

The Zoo

The children would like to visit the zoo.	Les enfants voudraient aller au zoo.
Is it open every day?	Est-ce que c'est ouvert tous les jours?
Is there a nature reserve?	Y a-t-il une réserve naturelle?
Can one drive through it?	Peut-on la traverser en voiture?

Where can we park the car?	**Où peut-on laisser la voiture?**
Where can one buy animal food?	**Où peut-on acheter de la nourriture pour les animaux?**
When is feeding time?	**A quelle heure donne-t-on à manger aux animaux?**
Can the children ride an elephant?	**Est-ce que les enfants peuvent monter sur un éléphant?**
Is there a children's zoo?	**Y a-t-il un zoo pour enfants?**

VOCABULARY

antelope	**l'antilope**
aquarium	**l'aquarium**
baboon	**le babouin**
bat	**la chauve-souris**
bird	**l'oiseau**
bison	**le bison**
cat	**le chat**
crocodile	**le crocodile**
dog	**le chien**
giraffe	**la girafe**
hippopotamus	**l'hippopotame**
horse	**le cheval**
hyena	**l'hyène**
leopard	**le léopard**
lion	**le lion**
rhinoceros	**le rhinocéros**
seal	**le phoque**
snake	**le serpent**
zebra	**le zèbre**

Sport

The French are keen on sport and the open air. They are
supporters of teams and of individuals who play football and
rugby. They follow the stars of the world of cycling and
attend race meetings with the same fervour as most people.

They also have their own particular sports. In the south
bullfighting is a spectator sport shared with Spain, but in the
Camargue there is an entirely original battle of wits against
bulls. This consists of attempts by agile young men to pin a
rosette between the horns of a frisky young bull.

Another sport played in the south-west is **pelote**. This is a
Basque game played by a team in a large court in which the
ball is batted against a wall with a long basket-like racquet
attached to the right hand. Another popular sport is
pétanque, a form of bowls which was played in the sixteenth
century. It takes place on an alley of beaten earth, usually in
village squares, where the game becomes an excuse for male
gatherings and much talking and wine drinking.

The French love of the open air and **culture physique** is
evident in the large number of excellent camping sites that
abound everywhere and the beach clubs for children and for
adults who want to keep in trim.

Football

Where is the stadium?	**Où est le stade?**
Could you show me the way to get there?	**Pouvez-vous m'indiquer le chemin pour y aller?**
Should I book tickets?	**Faut-il acheter des billets d'avance?**
Will it be very crowded?	**Y aura-t-il beaucoup de monde?**

Who is playing?	**Quelles sont les équipes?**
Is there a local team?	**Y a-t-il une équipe locale?**
I want a ticket for the main stand.	**Je voudrais un billet pour la tribune d'honneur.**
a place under cover/in the open.	**les gradins couverts/non couverts.**
I should like a programme.	**Je voudrais un programme.**

Vocabulary

attack	**l'attaque**
defence	**la défense**
goalkeeper	**le gardien de but**
goalposts	**les montants de but**
halfway line	**la ligne médiane**
penalty area	**la surface de réparation**
players	**les joueurs**
referee	**l'arbitre**
team	**l'équipe**

Race Meetings

I want a ticket for the paddock/a grandstand seat, please.	**Je voudrais un billet pour le paddock/pour une place à la tribune, s'il vous plaît.**
Where can I place a bet?	**Où fait-on les paris?**
What are the odds on number 5?	**Quelle est la cote du numéro cinq?**
Which is the favourite?	**Quel est le favori?**

Sport

I will back the outsider.	**Je veux miser sur le cheval non-classé.**
Is the jockey well-known?	**Est-ce que le jockey est bien connu?**

---

course	**le champs de courses**
filly	**la pouliche**
flat	**le plat**
horse	**le cheval**
hurdles	**les haies**
jockey	**le jockey**
owner	**le propriétaire**
photo finish	**la photo-finish**
rails	**la clôture**
stable	**l'écurie**
starting gate	**la barrière**
tote	**le totalisateur**
trainer	**l'entraîneur**

Tennis

Is there a tennis club near here?	**Y a-t-il un club de tennis près d'ici?**
Where is the championship held?	**Où se tiennent les championnats?**
How can I get some tickets?	**Comment peut-on obtenir des billets?**
Should I arrive early?	**Faut-il arriver de bonne heure?**
Who is playing?	**Qui sont les joueurs?**

Is it on hard courts or grass?	**Est-ce que c'est sur surface rapide ou sur gazon?**
I want to watch the men's singles/doubles/mixed doubles.	**Je voudrais voir le simple messieurs/double/double mixte.**
How do you score in French?	**Comment compte-t-on les points en français?**
15, 30, 40, deuce, advantage in/out, game, set, match.	**Quinze, trente, quarante, égalité, avantage service/dehors, jeu, set, match.**
Shall we toss for service?	**Allons-nous tirer au sort pour le service?**
Let's adjust the net.	**Ajustons le filet.**
It's too high/too low.	**Il est trop haut/trop bas.**
That was out/in/on the line.	**Cette balle était faute/bonne/sur la ligne.**
Good shot.	**Belle balle.**
Will you keep the score?	**Voulez-vous tenir la marque?**
Change ends.	**Changez de côté.**

VOCABULARY

backhand	**un revers**
forehand	**un coup droit**
racquet	**une raquette**
rally	**une belle passe de jeu**
spin	**un lift**
smash	**un smash**
tennis ball	**une balle de tennis**

Sport

| umpire | l'arbitre |
| volley | une volley |

Golf

Is there a golf course nearby?	Y a-t-il un terrain de golf près d'ici?
Does one have to be a member?	Faut-il être membre?
Is there temporary membership?	Peut-on devenir membre temporaire?
How much does it cost to play?	Combien faut-il payer pour jouer?
I'd like a caddy.	Je voudrais un caddie.
Are there any trolleys for hire?	Peut-on louer un chariot?
I'd like to speak to the professional.	Je voudrais parler au moniteur.
Can you give me a lesson now?	Pouvez-vous me donner une leçon maintenant?
Will you play a round with me?	Voulez-vous faire une tournée avec moi?
My handicap is eighteen.	J'ai dix-huit points de handicap.
I can't get any length on my drive.	Je ne trouve pas la bonne distance.
My approach shots are weak.	Mes coups d'approche sont faibles.
I'll do some putting while I wait for you.	Je m'exercerai à poter la balle pendant que je vous attends.

Can I hire some clubs?	**Puis-je louer des cannes?**
May I have a scorecard?	**Pouvez-vous me donner une carte du parcours?**

VOCABULARY

bunker	**la banquette**
birdie	**un coup sous la norme**
club house	**le club**
eagle	**deux coups sous la norme**
fairway	**le gazon**
golf bag	**le sac de golf**
green	**le green**
hook	**une balle de droite à gauche**
irons	**les fers**
mashie	**mashie**
niblick	**niblick**
par	**la normale du parcours**
rough	**l'herbe longue**
slice	**un coup qui fait dévier la balle**

Water-skiing

I have never skied before, not even on snow.	**Je n'ai jamais fait de ski, même pas sur de la neige.**
I am not a good swimmer.	**Je ne suis pas bon nageur.**
Do I wear a life jacket?	**Faut-il mettre un gilet de sauvetage?**
Will you please help me to put on the skis?	**Pouvez-vous m'aider à mettre les skis?**
Please pass me the rope.	**Pouvez-vous me passer la corde?**

Sport

May I ride on the speed boat?	**Est-ce que je peux monter dans le canot-automobile?**
Can I borrow a wetsuit?	**Est-ce que je peux emprunter une combinaison d'homme-grenouille?**
I'm ready now.	**Je suis prêt.**
Just a moment.	**Attendez un instant.**

VOCABULARY

aquaplane	**l'aquaplane**
bathing hat	**un bonnet de bain**
goggles	**des lunettes protectrices**
to jump	**sauter**
monoski	**le monoski**
slalom	**le slalom**

Riding

Is there a riding stable here?	**Y a-t-il un centre d'équitation ici?**
Can I hire a horse for riding?	**Est-ce que je peux louer un cheval pour faire de l'équitation?**
Do you give lessons?	**Donnez-vous des leçons?**
I'd like to go on a hack.	**Je voudrais faire du cheval.**
I'd like a quiet horse.	**Je voudrais un cheval paisible.**
Have you any ponies?	**Avez-vous des poneys?**

Will an instructor accompany the ride?	**Est-ce qu'un instructeur nous accompagnera?**
I'd like to practise jumping.	**Je voudrais pratiquer le saut.**
I am an experienced rider/a novice.	**J'ai l'habitude de faire du cheval/je suis un novice.**
Do you have English saddles?	**Avez-vous des selles anglaises?**
This horse has gone lame.	**Ce cheval boite.**
The girth is too loose.	**La sangle est trop lâche.**
Will you please adjust my stirrups/girth?	**Pouvez-vous ajuster mes étriers/ma sangle?**
Will you hold my horse while I get on?	**Pouvez-vous tenir mon cheval pendant que je monte?**
Will you give me a leg up?	**Voulez-vous m'aider à monter en selle?**

VOCABULARY

bit	**le mors**
bridle	**la bride**
girth	**la sangle**
harness	**le harnais**
hoof	**le sabot**
hock	**le jarret**
martingale	**le martingale**
mare	**la jument**
reins	**les rênes**
stallion	**l'étalon**
withers	**le garrot**

Fishing

Where can I get a permit to fish?	**Où peut-on obtenir un permis de pêche?**
Is there coarse fishing in this area?	**Peut-on pêcher des poissons ordinaires par ici?**
Are there any trout or salmon?	**Y a-t-il de la truite ou du saumon?**
How much does a day's fishing cost?	**Combien faut-il payer par jour?**
Is that per rod?	**Par ligne?**
Where can I get some bait?	**Où est-ce qu'on trouve de l'appât?**
Is there a minimum size that I am allowed to keep?	**Y a-t-il une taille minimum que je peux garder?**
What is the best time of day to go out?	**Quel est le meilleur moment de la journée pour pêcher?**
Are there any boats that will take me deep sea fishing?	**Y aurait-il un bateau pour m'emmener faire de la pêche en pleine mer?**
Do they provide tackle?	**Est-ce qu'ils fournissent l'attirail de pêche?**

VOCABULARY

fishing season	**pêche ouverte**
fly	**la mouche**
float	**le flotteur**
gaff	**la gaffe**
hook	**le hameçon**
line	**la ligne**

lure	**le leurre**
net	**le filet**
reel	**le moulinet**
spinner	**l'hélice**
weights	**les poids**

Shooting

Where can I shoot?	**Où est-ce que je peux chasser?**
Do I need a licence?	**Est-ce que j'ai besoin d'un permis?**
I'd like to borrow a 12-bore shotgun.	**Je voudrais emprunter un fusil de chasse de calibre douze.**
I have my own rifle.	**J'ai mon propre fusil.**
Is there a shooting party I could join?	**Est-ce que je pourrais participer à une partie de chasse?**
Is there a clay pigeon shoot?	**Y a-t-il un tir au pigeon artificiel?**
Is there a rifle range near?	**Y a-t-il un champ de tir près d'ici?**
When does the season for chamois begin?	**Quand est-ce que la saison du chamois commence?**

Vocabulary

barrel	**le canon**
backsight	**la hausse**
bullets	**les balles**

Sport

butt	la crosse
catch	attraper
cartridges	les cartouches
ejector	l'éjecteur
foresight	la mire
hammer	le chien
revolver	le révolver
safety catch	le cran de sûreté
trigger	la gâchette
telescopic sight	la visée télescopique

Sailing and Boating

I'd like to hire a dinghy.	Je voudrais louer un canot.
Is an outboard motor extra?	Est-ce qu'un moteur hors-bord est en plus?
Does this have an auxiliary engine?	Est-ce qu'il a un moteur auxiliaire?
How many berths are there?	Combien de couchettes y a-t-il?
How much water does it draw?	Quel est son tirant d'eau?
Is there a stove/sink/chemical toilet?	Y a-t-il un réchaud/un évier/des toilettes chimiques?
Are all cutlery, china and cooking utensils included?	Est-ce que les couverts, la vaisselle et les ustensiles de cuisine sont compris?
Have you got a map of the river?	Avez-vous une carte de la rivière?
Are there many locks to negotiate?	Faut-il passer par beaucoup d'écluses?

At what time do the locks close?	**A quelle heure ferment les écluses?**
How far is it to the next place where I can get some fuel?	**A quel distance d'ici peut-on acheter du carburant?**
Can I leave the boat here while we go to the shops?	**Est-ce que je peux laisser le bateau ici pendant que nous allons faire des courses?**
Where is the next refuse dump?	**Où est le dépotoir le plus proche?**
Will you please give me a tow?	**Pourriez-vous me remorquer?**

VOCABULARY

anchor	**l'ancre**
boat	**le bateau**
boathook	**la gaffe**
canoe	**le canoë**
chart	**la carte**
diesel engine	**un moteur diesel**
deck	**le pont**
fender	**la défense**
halyard	**la drisse**
hull	**la coque**
jib	**le foc**
keel	**la quille**
lifebelt	**la ceinture de sauvetage**
lifejacket	**le gilet de sauvetage**
motorboat	**la vedette**
mast	**le mât**
mainsail	**la grande voile**
oar	**la rame**
paddle	**l'aube**

Sport

pennant	**la flamme**
port (left)	**bâbord**
propeller	**l'hélice**
rowing boat	**le bateau à rame**
sail	**la voile**
starboard (right)	**tribord**
steer	**conduire**
stern	**la poupe**
tiller	**la barre**
yacht	**le yacht**

Winter Sports

The region where France and Switzerland meet is crowned by some of the highest Alps and a variety of skiing resorts, from the large traditional ones such as Chamonix to ultra-modern complexes like Flaine. On the Swiss side there are the smart resorts of Gstaad and Montana Crans. All the resorts are easy to reach, sometimes only a short car ride away from the lakeside, and they are much patronized by the local inhabitants, especially at weekends. Life at the resorts is cheerfully informal, with **après-ski** parties and moonlight sledge rides.

I'd like to join the class for beginners/intermediate skiers.	**Est-ce que je peux aller aux cours pour débutants/ skieurs moyens?**
Is there a beginners' slope?	**Y a-t-il une piste pour débutants?**

Where can I hire skis?
   a toboggan?
   boots?
   ski sticks?
	Où peut-on louer des skis?
	   une luge?
	   des chaussures?
	   des bâtons?

I have never skied before.	Je n'ai jamais fait de ski.
These boots are uncomfortable.	Ces chaussures ne sont pas confortables.
They are too tight/loose/big/small.	Elles sont trop serrées/lâches/grandes/petites.
How far is the ski hoist from the hotel?	A quelle distance de l'hôtel se trouve le remonte-pente?
Can I get a season ticket?	Peut-on acheter un abonnement?
Are the skiing conditions good this morning?	Est-ce que les conditions sont bonnes pour le ski ce matin?
Are all the pistes open?	Est-ce que toutes les pistes sont ouvertes?
Is there any cross-country skiing?	Peut-on faire du ski de fond?
Please help me up.	Pouvez-vous m'aider à me relever?
I think I've twisted my ankle.	Je crois que je me suis tordu la cheville.
May I join the midnight sledge party?	Est-ce que je peux participer à la partie de luge qui aura lieu à minuit?
Two entrance tickets for the ice rink.	Deux billets pour la patinoire.
Is there a heated swimming pool?	Y a-t-il une piscine chauffée?
Look out! I can't stop!	Attention! Je ne peux pas m'arrêter!

Sport

anorak	**l'anorak**
avalanche	**l'avalanche**
cable car	**la nacelle téléphérique**
funicular	**le funiculaire**
ice	**la glace**
ice skating	**le patinage**
slalom	**le slalom**
skates	**les patins**
ski-lift	**le remonte-pente**
snow	**la neige**
toboggan run	**la piste de toboggan**
waterproof trousers	**un pantalon imperméable**

General Services

If you are travelling independently or having a self-catering holiday at a villa or apartment, phrases for dealing with gas, electricity and plumbing problems will be indispensable. But even when all that is taken care of by someone else it is useful to be able to communicate with Post Office staff, telephone operators and other officials in their own language.

Post Office

Post Offices in France have the sign **P et T** outside them and their mail boxes are yellow, as they are in Switzerland. In Belgium letter-boxes are red. You can also buy stamps at tobacco kiosks which carry the red cigar-shaped sign for **tabac** (in France).

Is there a Post Office near here?	**Y a-t-il un Bureau de Postes près d'ici?**
What are the opening hours?	**Quelles sont les heures d'ouverture?**
Can I cash an international money order here?	**Est-ce que je peux toucher un mandat international ici?**
I want some stamps for a letter to Britain.	**Je veux des timbres pour une lettre pour l'Angleterre.**
What is the postcard postage rate for the USA?	**Combien de timbres faut-il sur les cartes pour les Etats-Unis?**
I'd like to register this letter.	**Je voudrais envoyer cette lettre en recommandé.**
I want to send it airmail. express. by surface rate. by printed matter rate.	**Je veux l'envoyer par avion. express. par voie de terre/de mer. comme imprimé.**

Where do I post parcels?	**Où est le guichet pour les paquets?**
Do I need a customs form?	**Est-ce qu'il faut une fiche pour la douane?**
Is there a poste restante here?	**Y a-t-il une poste restante ici?**
Have you a letter for me?	**Avez-vous une lettre pour moi?**
May I have a telegram form?	**Je voudrais un formulaire de télégramme.**
I'll send it by the cheap rate/ normal rate.	**Je l'enverrai au tarif réduit/ au tarif normal.**
When will it arrive?	**Quand est-ce qu'elle arrivera?**
I want to make a local telephone call.	**Je voudrais faire un appel téléphonique local.**
an international/person to person call.	**un appel international/ avec préavis.**
Can you reverse the charges?	**Je voudrais téléphoner en P.C.V.**
Switchboard, the line is engaged. Please try again later.	**La ligne est occupée. Rappellez plus tard.**

The Police Station

I am a visitor to your country.	**Je suis en visite dans votre pays.**
I would like to report a theft/loss/ accident/crime.	**Je voudrais signaler un vol/la perte d'un objet/un accident/ un crime.**

Someone stole my wallet.	**On m'a volé mon porte-feuille.**
Something was stolen from my car/my hotel room.	**On m'a volé quelque chose dans ma voiture/dans ma chambre.**
The theft occurred in the Rue de Paris at about four o'clock.	**Le vol a eu lieu dans la Rue de Paris vers quatre heures.**
I have lost my watch on the beach.	**J'ai perdu ma montre sur la plage.**
It is valuable.	**C'est un objet de valeur.**
It has sentimental value.	**Il a une valeur sentimentale.**
I will offer a reward.	**J'offrirai une récompense.**
Someone has been knocked down.	**Quelqu'un a été renversé par une voiture.**
A lady has broken her leg.	**Une dame s'est cassé la jambe.**
There is a man molesting women on the promenade.	**Il y a un homme sur l'esplanade qui importune les femmes.**
I have been swindled.	**J'ai été roulé.**
Can a police officer come with me?	**Est-ce qu'un agent peut venir avec moi?**
I will be a witness.	**Je veux bien être témoin.**
I cannot be a witness. I did not see what was happening.	**Je ne peux pas être temoin. Je n'ai pas vu ce qui s'est passé.**
Is there anyone who speaks English?	**Y a t-il quelqu'un qui parle l'anglais?**

Electricity

The lights have gone out.	**La lumière s'est éteinte.**
The power plug is not working.	**La prise ne marche pas.**
The fuse has gone.	**Les plombs ont sauté.**
I think it's the switch.	**Je crois que c'est l'interrupteur.**
There is a smell of burning.	**Ça sent le brulé.**
The stove won't light.	**La cuisinière ne s'allume pas.**
The heating has broken down.	**Le chauffage ne fonctionne pas.**
Can you mend it straight away?	**Pouvez-vous le réparer tout de suite?**
Where is the fuse box?	**Où est la boîte à fusible?**
Which is the main switch?	**Où est le disjoncteur?**

VOCABULARY

adaptor	**un raccord**
bulb	**une ampoule**
electric cooker	**une cuisinière électrique**
electric fire	**un feu électrique**
extensions lead	**une rallonge**
fuse wire	**le fusible**
hair dryer	**un sèche-cheveux**
insulating tape	**du chatterton**
iron	**un fer à repasser**
plug	**une prise**
radio	**un poste de radio**
razor point	**une prise pour rasoir**

refrigerator	un réfrigérateur
television	un poste de télévision
torch	une torche
water heater	un chauffe-eau

Gas

There is a smell of gas.	Ça sent le gaz.
It must be a gas leak.	Il doit y avoir une fuite.
This is the gas meter.	Voilà le compteur.
This gas jet won't light.	Le brûleur ne s'allume pas.
The pilot light keeps going out.	La veilleuse s'éteint toujours.
Is there any danger of an explosion?	Y a-t-il un risque d'explosion?
I think the ventilator is blocked.	Je crois que le ventilateur est bloqué.
We can't get any hot water.	Nous ne pouvons pas avoir d'eau chaude.

VOCABULARY

chimney	la cheminée
gas fire	le radiateur à gaz
gas light	la lumière à gaz
gas main	la conduite maîtresse
gas pipe	le tuyau du gaz
gas tap	le robinet du gaz
geyser	le chauffe-bain
hammer	le marteau
key	la clé
lagging	l'enveloppe isolante

| spanner | **la clé à écrous** |
| water heater | **le chauffe-eau** |

Plumbing

Are you the plumber?	**Etes-vous le plombier?**
The sink is stopped up.	**L'évier est bouché.**
There is a blockage in the pipe.	**Le tuyau est bouché.**
The tap needs a new washer.	**Il faut mettre une nouvelle rondelle au robinet.**
This water pipe is leaking.	**Ce tuyau a une fuite.**
The lavatory cistern won't fill.	**Le réservoir de chasse d'eau ne se remplit pas.**
The valve is stuck.	**La soupape est bloquée.**
The float is punctured.	**Le flotteur est perforé.**
The water tank has run dry.	**Le réservoir à eau est vide.**
The tank is overflowing.	**Le réservoir déborde.**

Vocabulary

basin	**le lavabo**
bath	**la baignoire**
cesspool	**la fosse d'aisances**
immersion heater	**le chauffe-eau électrique**
main water	**l'eau courante**
main drainage	**le tout-à-l'égout**
overflow pipe	**le trop-plein**
plug	**le bouchon**
stopcock	**le robinet d'arrêt**

Personal Services

This section suggests useful phrases for such occasions as a visit to a doctor, dentist, hairdresser, hospital or beautician.

At the Doctor's

Can you recommend a doctor?	**Pouvez-vous me conseiller un médecin?**
Is there an English-speaking doctor in the town?	**Y a-t-il un médecin qui parle l'anglais dans cette ville?**
Where is the surgery?	**Où est le cabinet de consultation?**
I have an appointment. My name is ...	**J'ai un rendez-vous. Je m'appelle ...**
Can the doctor come to the hotel/house?	**Est-ce que le médecin peut venir à l'hôtel/à la maison?**
I'm not feeling well.	**Je ne me sens pas bien.**
I feel sick.	**J'ai envie de vomir.**
I feel dizzy/shivery.	**J'ai des étourdissements/des frissons.**
I feel faint.	**Je me sens mal.**
The pain is here.	**J'ai mal ici.**
I have hurt my ...	**Je me suis fait mal à ...**

I have a temperature.
  a headache.
  back ache.
  sore throat.
  sunburn.
	**J'ai de la fièvre.
	  mal à la tête.
	  mal au dos.
	  mal à la gorge.
	  un coup de soleil.**

I have diarrhoea.	**J'ai de la diarrhée.**
I am constipated.	**Je suis constipé.**
I have been vomiting.	**J'ai vomi.**
I have been like this since yesterday.	**Je suis dans cet état depuis hier.**
Do you want me to undress?	**Voulez-vous que je me déshabille?**
Is it serious?	**C'est grave?**
Should I stay in bed?	**Est-ce que je dois rester au lit?**
Should I arrange to go home?	**Est-ce que je devrais faire le nécessaire pour rentrer en Angleterre?**
I am allergic to . . .	**Je suis allergique à . . .**
I have a heart condition.	**J'ai une maladie de coeur.**
I am asthmatic/diabetic.	**J'ai de l'asthme/du diabète.**
Do I have to pay for hospitalization and medicines?	**Est-ce que je dois payer l'hôpital et les médicaments?**
It's only a slight problem.	**Ce n'est qu'un petit problème.**

VOCABULARY

PARTS OF THE BODY

ankle	**la cheville**
appendix	**l'appendice**
arm	**le bras**
artery	**l'artère**

back	**le dos**
bladder	**la vessie**
blood	**le sang**
bone	**l'os**
bowels	**les intestins**
breast	**le sein**
cheek	**la joue**
chest	**la poitrine**
chin	**le menton**
collarbone	**la clavicule**
ear	**l'oreille**
elbow	**le coude**
eye	**l'oeil**
face	**le visage**
finger	**le doigt**
foot	**le pied**
forehead	**le front**
gland	**la glande**
hand	**la main**
heart	**le coeur**
heel	**le talon**
hip	**la hanche**
intestine	**l'intestin**
jaw	**la mâchoire**
joint	**l'articulation**
kidney	**le rein**
knee	**le genou**
leg	**la jambe**
lip	**la lèvre**
liver	**le foie**
lung	**le poumon**
mouth	**la bouche**
muscle	**le muscle**
neck	**le cou**
nerve	**le nerf**
nose	**le nez**
penis	**le pénis**

rib	**la côte**
shoulder	**l'épaule**
skin	**la peau**
spine	**la colonne vertébrale**
stomach	**l'estomac**
tendon	**le tendon**
testicle	**le testicule**
thigh	**la cuisse**
throat	**la gorge**
thumb	**le pouce**
toe	**l'orteil**
tongue	**la langue**
tonsils	**les amygdales**
urine	**l'urine**
vein	**la veine**
vagina	**le vagin**
wrist	**le poignet**
womb	**l'utérus**

INDISPOSITIONS

abscess	**un abcès**
asthma	**l'asthme**
bite (dog/insect)	**une morsure/piqûre**
blisters	**des ampoules**
boil	**un furoncle**
burn/scald	**une brûlure**
chill	**un refroidissement**
cold	**un rhume**
convulsions	**des convulsions**
cut	**une coupure**
diabetes	**le diabète**
diarrhoea	**la diarrhée**
dizziness	**le vertige**
haemorrhoids	**les hémorroïdes**
hay fever	**le rhume des foins**
indigestion	**une indigestion**

infection	une infection
inflammation	une inflammation
influenza	la grippe
irritation	une irritation
nausea	la nausée
rash	une éruption
rheumatism	le rhumatisme
shivers	des frissons
stiff neck	le torticolis
sunstroke	un coup de soleil
tonsillitis	une angine
ulcer	un ulcère
whooping cough	la coqueluche
wound	une plaie

At the Dentist's

I need an appointment as soon as possible.	Je voudrais un rendez-vous le plus vite possible.
I have a toothache/an abscess.	J'ai mal aux dents/un abcès.
Can you suggest a painkiller to take in the meantime?	Pouvez-vous me recommander un analgésique à prendre entre temps?
The bad tooth is at the front/back/side.	La dent qui me fait mal est devant/derrière/sur le côté.
Can you extract it?	Pouvez-vous l'arracher?
Does it need a filling?	Est-ce qu'il faut la plomber?
Can you put in a temporary filling?	Pouvez-vous faire un plombage provisoire?
Can I bite normally?	Est-ce que je peux manger normalement?

Personal Services

I'd prefer gas to an injection.	**Je préfère être anesthésié plutôt que d'avoir une piqûre.**
My gums are bleeding.	**Mes gencives saignent.**
I have broken my dentures.	**J'ai cassé mon dentier.**
What is your fee?	**Quel est votre tarif?**

At the Optician's

I have broken my glasses.	**J'ai cassé mes lunettes.**
Can you repair them temporarily?	**Pouvez-vous les réparer provisoirement?**
The lens is broken. Can you get a new one quickly?	**Le verre est cassé. Pouvez-vous le remplacer rapidement?**
Have you got contact lenses?	**Avez-vous des lentilles de contact?**
I'd like a pair of tinted spectacles.	**Je voudrais une paire de lunettes teintées.**
Do you sell binoculars/a magnifying glass/sunglasses?	**Vendez-vous des jumelles/ une loupe/des lunettes de soleil?**
I had better have an eye test.	**Il vaudrait mieux me faire examiner les yeux.**
I am short-sighted/long-sighted.	**Je suis myope/presbyte.**
How long will it take for my new glasses to be ready?	**Dans combien de temps mes nouvelles lunettes seront-elles prêtes?**
How much will they cost?	**Combien coûteront-elles?**

At the Chiropodist's

I have a painful corn.	**J'ai un cors qui me fait mal.**
Can you remove it?	**Pouvez-vous l'enlever?**
I have a bunion which is rubbing against my shoe.	**J'ai un oignon qui frotte contre la chaussure.**
I have a hard spot on the ball of my foot.	**J'ai un durillon sous le pied.**
My nails need attention. One of them is ingrowing.	**Mes ongles ont besoin de soins. J'ai un ongle incarné.**
Have you anything to soften them?	**Avez-vous quelque chose pour les adoucir?**
The soles of my feet are very sore.	**J'ai très mal à la plante des pieds.**

At the Hairdresser's

Where is the nearest hairdresser? Is there one in the hotel?	**Où est le salon de coiffure le plus proche? Y en a-t-il un à l'hôtel?**
I'd like to make an appointment.	**Je voudrais prendre rendez-vous.**
I want a cut and set.	**Je voudrais une coupe et une mise en plis.**
a shampoo and set.	** un shampooing et une mise en plis.**
I wear it brushed forward with a fringe.	**Je les coiffe vers l'avant avec une frange.**
I like it brushed back.	**Je les voudrais en arrière.**

Personal Services

Can you put some waves/curls in?	**Pouvez-vous me faire des ondulations/des boucles?**
Draw it back into a bun.	**Tirez mes cheveux en arrière et faites un chignon.**
Give me a colour rinse, please.	**Faites moi un shampooing colorant, s'il vous plaît.**
I think I will have it dyed.	**Je crois que je vais les faire teindre.**
Have you got a colour chart?	**Avez-vous une gamme des teintes?**
No hairspray, thank you.	**Pas de laque, s'il vous plaît.**
I'd like a manicure.	**Je voudrais une manicure.**
What is the name of this varnish?	**Comment s'appelle ce vernis?**

VOCABULARY

auburn	**châtain roux**
blonde	**blonde**
brunette	**brune**
dryer	**le séchoir**
ginger	**rousse**
hairnet	**un filet à cheveux**
hair pin	**une épingle**
scissors	**des ciseaux**
razor	**un rasoir**
styling	**une coupe**

At the Beauty Salon

I'd like a complete beauty treatment, please.	Je voudrais un traitement complet.
just a facial.	un massage facial seulement.
to change my make-up.	changer mon maquillage.
something more suitable for the seaside.	quelque chose qui convient mieux pour le bord de la mer.
something lighter in tone.	un ton plus clair.
a more open-air look.	un maquillage de plein-air.
something for the evening.	un maquillage pour le soir.
I have a delicate skin.	J'ai une peau délicate.
Can you please suggest a new eye make-up?	Pouvez-vous suggérer un nouveau maquillage pour les yeux?
I think that is too heavy.	Je crois que c'est trop lourd.
Have you any false eyelashes?	Avez-vous des cils artificiels?
Perhaps my eyebrows need plucking?	Mes sourcils ont peut-être besoin d'être épilés?
I'd like to see some new lipstick colours.	Je voudrais voir les nouveaux coloris de rouge à lèvres.

At the Laundry/Cleaner's

I'd like them washed/cleaned and pressed, please.	Je voudrais les faire laver/nettoyer et repasser à la vapeur.

Personal Services

Will this stain come out? It is a coffee/blood/grease/biro stain.	**Est-ce que cette tache peut s'ôter? C'est une tache de café/de sang/de graisse/de stylo à bille.**
Will you iron these shirts?	**Pouvez-vous repasser ces chemises?**
I will collect them tomorrow.	**Je viendrai les chercher demain.**
Do you deliver?	**Est-ce que vous livrez à domicile?**
Do you do mending?	**Faites-vous le raccommodage?**
This tear needs patching.	**Cet accroc a besoin d'être rapiécé.**
Can you sew this button on?	**Pouvez-vous coudre ce bouton?**
Can you mend this invisibly?	**Pouvez-vous faire stopper ceci?**
This blouse/coat/dress is not mine.	**Ce chemisier/manteau/cette robe n'est pas à moi.**
My trousers are missing.	**Il manque mon pantalon.**
This was not torn when I brought it to you.	**Ceci n'était pas déchiré quand je vous l'ai apporté.**
How long does the launderette stay open?	**Jusqu'à quelle heure est-ce que la laverie est ouverte?**

VOCABULARY

bleach	**l'eau de Javel**
clothes hanger	**un cintre**

launderette	**la laverie automatique**
soap powder	**la poudre de savon**
washing machine	**la machine à laver**
water, hot/warm/cold	**l'eau très chaude/chaude/froide**

At the Men's Hairdresser's

I want a haircut, please.	**Une coupe de cheveux, s'il vous plaît.**
Just a trim, please. I haven't much time.	**Simplement rafraîchir, s'il vous plaît. Je suis pressé.**
Please give me a shampoo.	**Un shampooing, s'il vous plaît.**
I would like it cut shorter.	**Pouvez-vous les couper plus court?**
Leave it long, please.	**Laissez-les longs, s'il vous plaît.**
You are taking too much off.	**Vous en coupez trop.**
Take a little more off the back/sides/top.	**Un peu plus court derrière/sur les côtés/sur le dessus.**
I part my hair on the left/right.	**J'ai la raie à gauche/à droite.**
I'd like an alcohol rub/a singe.	**Je voudrais une friction à l'alcool/un brûlage de la pointe des cheveux.**
Please give me a shave.	**C'est pour la barbe.**
Could you trim my beard/moustache/sideboards?	**Pourriez-vous me rafraîchir la barbe/la moustache/les favoris?**
No thank you. I do not want a facial massage.	**Non merci, pas de massage facial.**

Personal Services

I will have a manicure.	**Une manucure, s'il vous plaît.**
May I have a hand towel?	**Pouvez-vous me donner une serviette?**
Put some eau de cologne on but no cream.	**Mettez de l'eau de cologne mais pas de crème.**
Move the mirror a bit more to the right/left.	**Tenez la glace un peu plus vers la droite/la gauche.**
Yes, that's fine.	**Oui, c'est très bien.**

Making Friends

Good morning/good afternoon/good evening. | **Bonjour/bonjour/bonsoir.**

May I introduce myself/my friend John/my wife? | **Vous permettez que je me présente/que je présente mon ami John/ma femme?**

My name is ... | **Je m'appelle ...**

How do you do? | **Enchanté.**

Are you staying at this hotel/at this resort? | **Vous êtes dans cet hôtel/dans cette ville?**

Are you enjoying your holiday? | **Etes-vous contents de vos vacances?**

How long have you been on holiday? | **Depuis quand êtes-vous en vacances?**

Do you always come here? | **Venez-vous toujours ici?**

I'd like you to meet my friend ... | **Je voudrais vous présenter mon ami ...**

Would you care to have a drink with us? | **Est-ce que je peux vous inviter à prendre quelque chose avec nous?**

What would you like? | **Qu'est-ce que vous prendrez?**

Please, I insist that you let me. | **C'est moi qui paie. J'insiste.**

I'm afraid that I don't speak French very well. | **Malheureusement je ne parle pas bien le français.**

It is very nice to talk to a French person. | **C'est bien agréable de parler à un Français/une Française.**

Which part of France do you come from? | **De quelle région de France êtes-vous?**

I am here with my wife/husband/family/friend(s).	**Je suis ici avec ma femme/avec mon mari/en famille/avec mon ami (mes amis).**
Are you alone?	**Etes-vous seul?**
We come from Manchester/England.	**Nous sommes de Manchester/d'Angleterre.**
Have you been to England?	**Etes-vous déjà allé en Angleterre?**
If you come, please let me know.	**Si vous y allez, prévenez-moi.**
This is my address.	**Voilà mon adresse.**
I hope to see you again soon.	**J'espère vous revoir bientôt.**
Perhaps we could meet for a drink after dinner?	**Nous pourrions peut-être prendre un verre ensemble après le dîner?**
I would be delighted to join you.	**Je serais très content de me joindre à vous.**
At what time shall I come?	**A quelle heure faut-il venir?**
Have you got a family?	**Avez-vous des enfants?**
Would you like to see some photos of our house and our children?	**Aimeriez-vous voir des photos de notre maison et de nos enfants?**
Are you going to the gala?	**Allez-vous au gala?**
Would you like to make up a party?	**Aimeriez-vous vous joindre à nous?**
It has been very nice to meet you.	**Je suis très content d'avoir fait votre connaissance.**
You have been very kind.	**Vous avez été très gentil.**

Dating Someone

Are you on holiday?	**Etes-vous en vacances?**
Do you live here?	**Habitez-vous ici?**
Do you like this place?	**Vous vous plaisez ici?**
I've just arrived.	**Je viens d'arriver.**
What is there to do?	**Qu'est-ce qu'on peut faire ici?**
I don't know anyone here.	**Je ne connais personne ici.**
I'm with a group of students.	**Je suis avec un groupe d'étudiants.**
I'm travelling alone.	**Je voyage seul.**
I'm on my way round Europe.	**Je fais le tour de l'Europe.**
I come from Scotland/Australia/New Zealand.	**Je viens d'Ecosse/d'Australie/de Nouvelle-Zélande.**
Do you mind if I try my French on you?	**Etes-vous d'accord pour que je pratique mon français avec vous?**
My French is not very good.	**Je ne parle pas bien le français.**
Would you like a drink?	**Aimeriez-vous prendre quelque chose?**
What are you doing this evening?	**Que faites-vous ce soir?**
Would you like to go to a discotheque?	**Aimeriez-vous aller à une discothèque?**
join our party?	**vous joindre à nous?**
Do you like dancing/concerts/opera?	**Aimez-vous danser/les concerts/l'opéra?**

Making Friends

Can I walk along with you?	**Est-ce que je peux vous accompagner?**
Which way are you going?	**De quel côté allez-vous?**
Do you mind if I sit here?	**Vous voulez bien que je m'assois ici?**
This is my friend, Tom.	**Je vous présente mon ami Tom.**
Do you have a girl friend?	**Avez-vous une petite amie?**
We could make a foursome.	**Nous pourrions sortir à quatre.**
Do you play tennis/golf?	**Vous jouez au tennis/au golf?**
Do you go swimming?	**Vous nagez?**
Which beach do you go to?	**A quelle plage allez-vous?**
Would you like to come for a drive/a boat ride?	**Aimeriez-vous faire un tour en voiture/en bateau?**
It would be nice if you would.	**Cela me ferait plaisir que vous veniez.**
Thanks for coming out with me.	**Merci d'être sorti avec moi.**
I enjoyed it.	**Cela m'a beaucoup plu.**
Can we meet again?	**Puis-je vous revoir?**
How about tomorrow?	**Demain?**
No thanks. I'm busy.	**Non merci. Je suis occupée.**
Please stop bothering me.	**Laissez-moi tranquille.**

Mutual Interest

Do you play cards?	**Vous jouez aux cartes?**

Would you like to make a four at bridge?	**Aimeriez-vous vous joindre à nous pour jouer au bridge?**
We play canasta/poker/rummy.	**Nous jouons au canasta/au poker/au 'rummy'.**
It is an English game.	**C'est un jeu anglais.**
Are you a chess player?	**Jouez-vous aux échecs?**
I'll ask the concierge if the hotel has a chess board.	**Je vais demander au concierge si l'hôtel dispose d'un jeu d'échec.**
This is your king/queen/knight/bishop/castle/pawn.	**Voilà votre roi/reine/cavalier/fou/tour/pion.**
We could play draughts or dominoes.	**Nous pourrions jouer aux dames ou aux dominos.**
We can play table tennis in the hotel. What do you say?	**On peut jouer au ping-pong à l'hôtel. Ça vous dit?**
Do you read English?	**Lisez-vous l'anglais?**
Would you like to borrow this book/newspaper?	**Voulez-vous emprunter ce livre/ce journal?**

Conversations

There are certain universal subjects of conversation which provide a bridge for communication with strangers all over the world. Among these are the weather, families, home, the cost of living and pets.

The following conversational phrases are designed to start you off on an acquaintanceship with people who do not speak English.

About the Weather

It is a fine day.	**Il fait beau.**
It's not a very nice day.	**Il ne fait pas très beau.**
Will it rain all day/later/tomorrow, do you think?	**Pensez-vous qu'il pleuvra toute la journée/plus tard/demain?**
It's going to be hot/cold today.	**Il va faire chaud/froid aujourd'hui.**
It's rather windy.	**Il y a pas mal de vent.**
I think there is a thunderstorm coming.	**Je crois qu'un orage se prépare.**
Look at the lightning.	**Regardez les éclairs.**
It will soon clear up.	**Ça va bientôt s'éclaircir.**
We don't get this kind of weather at home.	**Nous n'avons pas de temps pareil chez nous.**
It's a pity it is so dull.	**C'est dommage que le temps soit si couvert.**
Did you see the beautiful sunrise/sunset?	**Avez-vous vu le beau lever de soleil/coucher de soleil?**
We had a very good/very poor summer last year.	**Il a fait très beau/très mauvais l'été dernier.**
There's a lot of haze about today.	**Le temps est brumeux aujourd'hui.**
The atmosphere is very clear.	**Le temps est très clair.**
Is it cold here in the winter?	**Est-ce qu'il fait froid ici en hiver?**
I love the spring/summer/autumn.	**J'aime le printemps/l'été/l'automne.**

Vocabulary

breeze	la brise
cloudburst	l'averse
cloudy	nuageux
drizzle	le crachin
dry	sec
forecast	les prévisions de la météo
hail	la grêle
meteorological office	la météo
mist	la brume
office	le bureau
pressure	la pression
rain	la pluie
sleet	le grésil
snow	la neige
sunny	ensoleillé
temperature	la température
weather report	le bulletin météorologique

About Familes

This is my wife/husband/daughter/son.	Voilà ma femme/mon mari/ma fille/mon fils.
My son is an architect/doctor/student/teacher/engineer.	Mon fils est architecte/médecin/étudiant/professeur/ingénieur.
My daughter is at school.	Ma fille est écolière/lycéenne.
She is taking her examinations.	Elle passe ses examens.
Then she will go to university.	Ensuite elle ira à l'Université.
teacher's training college.	à l'Ecole Normale.
art school.	elle fera les Beaux-Arts.

Making Friends

She learned some French at school.	Elle a étudié le français à l'école.
My wife is Scottish.	Ma femme est écossaise.
My father was a teacher.	Mon père était professeur.
The children prefer to have holidays on their own.	Les enfants préfèrent partir en vacances sans nous.
They prefer camping.	Ils préfèrent le camping.
My youngest/eldest son	Mon plus jeune fils/mon fils aîné
My youngest/eldest daughter is married and lives in . . .	Ma plus jeune fille/ma fille aînée est mariée et habite à . . .
Would you like to see some photos of our family?	Voulez-vous voir des photos de la famille?
The younger children stayed at home with their grandparents.	Nos plus jeunes enfants sont restés à la maison avec leurs grands-parents.
Are these your children?	Ce sont vos enfants?
The boy/girl looks like his/her mother/father.	Le garçon/la fille ressemble à sa mère/à son père.
How old is he?	Quel âge a-t-il?
My daughter is fourteen.	Ma fille a quatorze ans.

VOCABULARY

birthday	l'anniversaire
aunt	la tante
cousin	le cousin/la cousine
divorce	le divorce
in-laws	les beaux-parents
marriage	le mariage

relatives	**la famille**
uncle	**l'oncle**
wedding	**le mariage**

About Homes

We have a house in town/in the country.	**Nous avons une maison en ville/à la campagne.**
It is a detached two-storey house.	**C'est une maison séparée à deux étages.**
a semi-detached house.	**une maison jumelle.**
a cottage.	**une petite maison de campagne.**
a maisonette.	**un duplex.**
a flat.	**un appartement.**
We have a large garden/a patio.	**Nous avons un grand jardin/ une terrasse.**
There are two living rooms. One has a French window and the other a bay window.	**Il y a deux salles de séjour. L'une a une porte-fenêtre, l'autre une fenêtre en baie.**
There is a fireplace in the dining room.	**Il y a une cheminée dans la salle à manger.**
(All) the house is centrally heated.	**Nous avons le chauffage central dans (toute) la maison.**
It is air conditioned.	**Elle est climatisée.**
We have two garages.	**Nous avons deux garages.**
The back garden has a lawn and a swimming pool.	**Le jardin derrière la maison a un gazon et une piscine.**
In our village there are many old houses.	**Dans notre village il y a beaucoup de vieilles maisons.**

Making Friends

We prefer a modern house.	**Nous préférons une maison moderne.**
What kind of house have you got?	**Quelle sorte de maison avez-vous?**
I like French-style houses.	**J'aime les maisons de style français.**
Do you cook by gas or electricity?	**Cuisinez-vous au gaz ou à l'électricité?**
In a warm climate tiled floors are delightful.	**Dans les pays chauds le carrelage est très agréable.**
Wall-to-wall carpeting makes a house warm in winter.	**La moquette rend la maison bien confortable en hiver.**
Built-in cupboards make a room seem larger.	**Des placards font paraître une pièce plus grande.**
Old furniture is lovely but very expensive.	**Les meubles anciens sont très beaux mais très chers.**

VOCABULARY

balcony	**le balcon**
brick	**la brique**
ceiling	**le plafond**
chimney	**la cheminée**
door	**la porte**
drains	**les égouts**
foundations	**les fondements**
gable	**le pignon**
mains electricity	**l'électricité**
gas	**le gaz de ville**
water	**l'eau courante**
plumbing	**la plomberie**
roof	**le toit**

terrace	la terrasse
tiles	le carrelage
wall	le mur
window	la fenêtre
window frame	l'encadrement de fenêtre
window pane	la vitre
wood	le bois

On Business

I have an appointment with the manager.	J'ai rendez-vous avec le directeur.
I am from Smith and Company.	Je viens de la part de Smith et Compagnie.
Here is my card.	Voilà ma carte.
It is good of you to see me.	Vous êtes bien aimable de me recevoir.
May I show you our catalogue/samples?	Vous permettez que je vous montre notre catalogue/nos échantillons?
My company manufactures knitwear.	Ma société fabrique des tricots.
We are looking for agents.	Nous cherchons des représentants.
Our wholesale/retail prices are on this list.	Nos prix de gros/de détail sont sur cette liste.
There is a special discount for a large quantity.	Nous faisons une remise spéciale sur les grosses commandes.
Delivery is within two months/immediate.	La livraison se fait dans les deux mois/immédiatement.

On Business

The prices are f.o.b.	Les prix sont franco à bord.
I would like to see your products.	Je voudrais voir vos produits.
Have you a showroom in the town?	Avez-vous un magasin d'exposition en ville?
What are your terms of business?	Quelles sont vos conditions?
Do you already have an agent in my country?	Avez-vous déjà un représentant dans mon pays?
Can you make modifications to this model?	Pouvez-vous apporter des modifications à ce modèle?
May I take some samples with me?	Est-ce que je peux emporter quelques échantillons?
I will give you an order now.	Je vais passer commande maintenant.
Can you look after the packing and shipping?	Pouvez-vous vous occuper de l'emballage et de l'expédition par bateau?
There is only a small market for these goods.	Il n'y a pas beaucoup de débouchés pour ces marchandises.

Vocabulary

banker	le banquier
balance sheet	le bilan
bill	la facture
bill of exchange	la traite
clerk	l'employé
credit	le crédit

contract	**le contrat**
correspondence	**la correspondance**
certificate	**le certificat**
draft	**le projet de contrat**
debit	**le débit**
export	**l'exportation**
freight	**le transport de marchandises**
insurance	**l'assurance**
import	**l'importation**
invoice	**la facture**
merchant	**le marchant**
receipt	**le reçu**
remittance	**la remise**
sale	**la vente**
warehouse	**l'entrepôt**

Looking After your Money

The Bank

Where is the nearest bank?	**Où est la banque la plus proche?**
Do you accept travellers' cheques?	**Acceptez-vous les chèques de voyage?**
Can I use a Eurocheque card?	**Est-ce que je peux me servir d'une carte Eurochèque?**
Do you issue money against a credit card?	**Est-ce qu'on peut toucher de l'argent avec une carte de crédit?**
I am expecting a remittance.	**On doit me faire une remise.**
I have a letter of credit.	**J'ai une lettre de crédit.**
I would like a draft to send away.	**Je voudrais un chèque bancaire à expédier.**
What is the rate of exchange for the pound/dollar/Australian dollar?	**Quel est le taux de change de la livre/du dollar/du dollar australien?**
What is your commission charge?	**Combien de commission prenez-vous?**
I will have it all in 100 franc notes.	**Donnez-le moi en billets de cent francs.**
Please give me ten francs worth of change.	**Donnez-moi de la monnaie pour dix francs.**
Can you split this cheque into several currencies?	**Pouvez-vous diviser ce chèque en plusieurs devises?**

I will have some German marks, Swiss francs and Italian lire.	**Je voudrais des marks allemands, des francs suisse et des lires italiennes.**
Can I open a temporary bank account?	**Est-ce que je peux ouvrir un compte provisoire?**
Can you arrange for some money to be sent from my bank in Britain?	**Pouvez-vous faire venir de l'argent de mon compte en banque en Angleterre?**
I seem to be ten francs short. Can you please count it again?	**Je crois qu'il me manque dix francs. Pouvez-vous recompter cet argent?**
Have you a card showing current exchange rates?	**Avez-vous une carte avec les taux du change actuels?**

Vocabulary

Bank of England	**la Banque d'Angleterre**
cashier	**le caissier**
cheque book	**le carnet de chèque**
credit	**le crédit**
coins	**les pièces**
deposit slip	**la feuille de dépôt**
debit	**le débit**
foreign exchange regulations	**les règlements de change extérieur**
manager	**le directeur**
notes	**les billets**
treasury	**la trésorerie**
signature	**la signature**

Coins: 1, 5, 10, 50 centimes
      1, 5, 10 francs
Notes: 10, 50, 100, 500 francs

Bureau de Change

Are you open outside banking hours?	**Etes-vous ouverts en dehors des heures d'ouverture des banques?**
Does the rate of exchange alter outside normal hours?	**Est-ce que le taux de change est différent en dehors des heures normales?**
Are you open on Sundays?	**Etes-vous ouverts le dimanche?**
Can you show me your rates of exchange?	**Pouvez-vous me montrer vos taux de change?**
Do you give the same rate for notes as for travellers' cheques?	**Le taux est-il le même pour les billets que pour les chèques de voyage?**

On Losing Travellers' Cheques or Credit Cards

When this happens you should immediately notify the company that has issued the cheques or card but you may need help from a local hotelier or banker.

I have lost my travellers' cheques/credit card.	**J'ai perdu mes chèques de voyage/ma carte de crédit.**
May I ask them to communicate with me through you?	**Est-ce que je peux leur donner votre nom pour qu'ils puissent entrer en communication avec moi?**
Have you a British representative?	**Avez-vous un représentant britannique?**

I hope they will be able to refund the cheques quickly. I have no other money.

J'espère qu'ils pourront me rembourser les chèques rapidement. Je n'ai pas d'autre argent.

I will ask my bank at home to send some money to you.

Je vais demander à ma banque chez moi de vous envoyer de l'argent.

Will you accept a British cheque in payment of the hotel bill?

Acceptez-vous un chèque britannique pour payer la note d'hôtel?

Reference Section

Numbers

1	un
2	deux
3	trois
4	quatre
5	cinq
6	six
7	sept
8	huit
9	neuf
10	dix
11	onze
12	douze
13	treize
14	quatorze
15	quinze
16	seize
17	dix-sept
18	dix-huit
19	dix-neuf
20	vingt
21	vingt et un
22	vingt-deux
23	vingt-trois
24	vingt-quatre
25	vingt-cinq
26	vingt-six
27	vingt-sept
28	vingt-huit
29	vingt-neuf
30	trente
40	quarante
50	cinquante

60	**soixante**
70	**soixante-dix**
80	**quatre-vingts**
90	**quatre-vingt dix**
100	**cent**
101	**cent un**
110	**cent dix**
200	**deux cents**
1000	**mille**
1001	**mille et un**
1100	**onze cent**
2000	**deux mille**
1,000,000	**un million**
1,000,000,000	**un milliard**

first	**premier**
second	**second/deuxième**
third	**troisième**
fourth	**quatrième**
fifth	**cinquième**
sixth	**sixième**
seventh	**septième**
eighth	**huitième**
ninth	**neuvième**
tenth	**dixième**

once	**une fois**
twice	**deux fois**
three times	**trois fois**

a half	**une moitié/un demi**
a quarter	**un quart**
a third	**un tiers**
an eighth	**un huitième**

a pair of	**une paire de**
a dozen	**une douzaine de**

173

Time

Greenwich Mean Time	G.M.T./T.U. (temps universel)
Central European time	l'heure de l'Europe Centrale
Atlantic time	l'heure de l'Atlantique
Date line	ligne de changement de date
am/pm	du matin/du soir
24 hour clock	horaire de vingt-quatre heures
summertime	l'heure d'été
It is 12.15	Il est douze heures quinze
12.20	vingt
12.30	trente
12.35	trente-cinq
12.45	quarante-cinq
1.00	treize heures
Midnight	minuit
Midday	midi

Phrases Referring to Time

What time is it?	Quelle heure est-il?
It is late.	Il est tard.
It is early.	Il est tôt.
Are we on time?	Sommes-nous à l'heure?
At what time shall we meet?	A quelle heure nous verrons-nous?
At what time are we expected?	A quelle heure sommes-nous attendus?
On the hour.	A l'heure.
Day by day.	De jour en jour.
By the minute.	Par minute.
Every second.	Chaque seconde.
At regular intervals.	A intervales réguliers.
After the clock strikes.	Quand l'horloge aura sonné.

days	**les jours**
weeks	**les semaines**
years	**les années**
Sunday	**dimanche**
Monday	**lundi**
Tuesday	**mardi**
Wednesday	**mercredi**
Thursday	**jeudi**
Friday	**vendredi**
Saturday	**samedi**
daybreak	**le lever du jour**
dawn	**l'aurore**
morning	**le matin**
afternoon	**l'après-midi**
evening	**le soir**
night	**la nuit**
today	**aujourd'hui**
yesterday	**hier**
tomorrow	**demain**
the day before yesterday	**avant-hier**
two days ago	**il y a deux jours**
the day after tomorrow	**après-demain**
the following day	**le jour suivant**
weekday	**jour de semaine**
a day off	**un congé**
birthday	**l'anniversaire**
Christmas Day	**le Jour de Noël**
New Year's Day	**le Jour de l'An**
All Saints' Day	**la Toussaint**
May Day	**le premier mai**
weekend	**le weekend**
last week	**la semaine dernière**
next week	**la semaine prochaine**
for two weeks	**pour deux semaines**
January	**janvier**
February	**février**
March	**mars**

April	**avril**
May	**mai**
June	**juin**
July	**juillet**
August	**août**
September	**septembre**
October	**octobre**
November	**novembre**
December	**décembre**
calendar month	**un mois au calendrier**
lunar month	**un mois lunaire**
monthly	**mensuel**
since January	**depuis janvier**
last month	**le mois dernier**
next month	**le mois prochain**
the month before	**le mois précédent**
the first of March	**le premier mars**
Spring	**le printemps**
Summer	**l'été**
Autumn	**l'automne**
Winter	**l'hiver**
years	**ans/années**
BC/AD	**Avant J.C./Après J.C.**
leap year	**année bissextile**

Temperature Equivalents

FAHRENHEIT		CENTIGRADE
212	Boiling point	100
100		37·8
98·4	Body temperature	37
86		30
77		25
68		20
50		10
32	Freezing point	0
0		−18

To convert Fahrenheit to Centigrade subtract 32 and divide by 1·8.

To convert Centigrade to Fahrenheit multiply by 1·8 and add 32.

Pressure

The barometer tells you the air pressure of the atmosphere: 15 lb. per sq. in. is normal air pressure at sea level. This equals 1·1 kg. per sq. cm.

A tyre gauge tells you the pressure of your car tyres.

POUNDS PER SQUARE INCH	KILOGRAMS PER SQUARE CENTIMETRE
16	1·12
18	1·27
20	1·41
22	1·55
24	1·69
26	1·83
28	1·97

Measurements of Distance

One kilometre = 1000 metres = 0·62 miles

One hundred centimetres = 1 metre = 3·3 ft.

One centimetre = 0·39 inches.

The following table gives equivalents for metres and feet. The figure in the centre column can stand for either feet or metres and the equivalent should then be read off in the appropriate column.

METRES	METRES AND FEET	FEET
0·30	1	3·28
0·61	2	6·56
0·91	3	9·84
1·22	4	13·12
1·52	5	16·40
1·83	6	19·68
2·13	7	22·97
2·44	8	26·25
2·74	9	29·53
3·05	10	32·81
3·35	11	36·09
3·66	12	39·37
3·96	13	42·65
4·27	14	45·93
4·57	15	49·21
4·88	16	52·49
5·18	17	55·77
5·49	18	59·05
5·79	19	62·34
6·10	20	65·62
7·62	25	82·02
15·24	50	164·04
22·86	75	264·06
30·48	100	328·08

MILES	MILES AND KILOMETRES	KILOMETRES
0·62	1	1·61
1·24	2	3·22
1·86	3	4·82
2·49	4	6·44
3·11	5	8·05
3·73	6	9·66
4·35	7	11·27
4·97	8	12·88
5·59	9	14·48
6·21	10	16·09
15·53	25	40·23
31·07	50	80·47
46·60	75	120·70
62·14	100	160·93

For motorists it is useful to remember that:

30 miles = 48·3 km.
70 miles = 112·7 km.
70 km. = 43·75 miles
100 km. = 62·50 miles

To convert kilometres to miles, divide by 8 and multiply by 5.

To convert miles to kilometres, divide by 5 and multiply by 8.

Measurements of Quantity

Weight

POUNDS	POUNDS AND KILOGRAMS	KILOGRAMS
2·20	1	0·45
4·40	2	0·90
6·61	3	1·36
8·81	4	1·81
11·02	5	2·27
13·23	6	2·72
15·43	7	3·18
17·64	8	3·63

OUNCES	GRAMS
0·5	14·12
1	28·35
2	56·70
3	85·05
4	113·40
5	141·75
6	170·10
7	198·45
8 ($\frac{1}{2}$ lb)	226·80
12	340·19
16 (1 lb)	453·59

One kilogram = 1000 grams = 2·2 lb.

Half a kilogram = 500 grams = 1·1 lb.

When shopping for small items, French people usually order by the 100 grams; this is about $3\frac{1}{2}$ ounces.

One metric ton = 1000 kilograms.

Liquid Measures

U.K. PINTS	U.K. PINTS AND LITRES	LITRES
1·76	1	0·57
3·52	2 (1 quart)	1·14
5·28	3	1·70
7·04	4	2·27
8·80	5	2·84
10·56	6	3·41
12·32	7	3·98
14·08	8 (1 gallon)	4·55
15·84	9	5·11
17·60	10	5·68

1 litre = 1·76 pints.

One tenth of a litre is a decilitre or ·18 of a pint.

One hundredth of a litre is a centilitre or ·018 of a pint.

One hundred litres are a hectolitre or 22 gallons.

One gallon = 4·6 litres.

One quart = 1·14 litres.

One pint = 0·57 litres.

Clothing Sizes

Measurements for clothes are measured according to the metric system in France. Here are the equivalent sizes for the main articles of clothing:

Women

DRESSES AND COATS

British	34	36	38	40	42	44	46
American	32	34	36	38	40	42	44
Continental	40	43	44	46	48	50	52

Men

SUITS

British and American	36	38	40	42	44	46
Continental	46	48	50	52	54	56

SHIRTS

British and American	14	14½	15	15½	16	16½	17
Continental	36	37	38	39	41	42	43

Index

Index